METROPOLITAN
manifesto

On Being the Counselor to the King in a Pluralistic Empire

Richard BLEDSOE

Theopolis™
BOOKS
AN IMPRINT OF ATHANASIUS PRESS

Metropolitan Manifesto: On Being the Counselor to the King in a Pluralistic Empire

Copyright © 2015 Theopolis Books
An Imprint of Athanasius Press

224 Auburn Avenue
Monroe, Louisiana 71201
www.athanasiuspress.org

ISBN: 978-0-9862924-1-5 (softcover)

Dedicated to my friend Jim Jordan, who gave me a number of the seed ideas for city work, especially from his remarkable commentary on Daniel.

TABLE OF CONTENTS

Preface

*...of the sons of Issachar who had understanding of the
times, to know what Israel ought to do....*
I Chronicles 12:32

*But I have heard it said of you that you can understand a
dream to interpret it....*
Genesis 41:15

*And the king said to them, "I have had a dream, and my
spirit is anxious to know is to know the dream."*
Daniel 2:3

*I thought it good to declare the signs and wonders that the
Most High God has worked for me. How great are His
signs, and how mighty His wonders!*
Daniel 4:2-3

"Sometimes after one of these meetings, I feel like I'm
on Mars or Venus, and not in our city." So said one of the
elder pastors, a chief among the city's pastors. We had just
met with an official from our very liberal and progressive
city. This official had just left, but not before we sat him in a
chair and had the pastors of the city gather 'round him, lay

hands on him, pray for him and bless him. The remarkable thing is that almost all of these officials want to come and see us again.

THE STATEMENT OF THE CHALLENGE AND THE OPPORTUNITY

Things are not as simple as once hoped. With the Reformation, there was a collapse of a unified Christendom and the rise of a new order of secular nation-states that did not have a theological foundation. A new foundation had to be discovered that was regarded as self evident and universally recognizable. We now live in a pluralistic world that has made naturalism its default metaphysical foundation. Naturalism, however, is not self grounding or self evident and must itself account for its own grounding and origins.[1] This oddly is very similar to the Ancient world that saw the triumph of Christianity as the answer to its own insoluble problems. Ancient pluralistic empires were grounded in many gods. The gods themselves emerged somehow from the background of metaphysical chaos, and the gods that emerged were in conflict with one another. Today, pluralism seeks its foundation in Darwinism, and Darwinism likewise believes that all current order and life somehow emerged out of the background of chemical and biological chaos, which are likewise at war with one another for survival. Ancient and modern pluralistic empires have analogous dilemmas.

---

1 C. S. Lewis saw this dilemma with striking clarity, and in a masterpiece of compressed exposition exposes the internal self contradiction of naturalism in the third chapter of his book, Miracles, p. 17-24. *Miracles: A Preliminary Study*, Lewis, C. S. (1969), United States of America, The Macmillan Company.

The Bible speaks to modern pluralism just as it spoke to ancient pluralism. Truth that gives orientation to public officials is a challenge in both settings. Pluralism, either ancient or modern, cannot give rise to any coherent idea of truth. Ancient political problems are not so far from modern political problems.

We must re-introduce truth back into the public square. There is a new kind of bishop and counselor who represents the Church as a whole who can do this. I myself re-discovered this. There is a place and a way for a single pastor to function as a "re-introducer" of the truth of the Gospel and of the Living God in a modern pluralistic situation that does not recognize a singular truth. The role of counselor and advisor in the name of Jesus Christ to those in authority is a living possibility. I know. I have been a part of this in my own city, and I have done it.

Chapter One

ADVISOR TO THE KING: THE PERSONAL BACKGROUND

In 1990 I received a call from my friend, the pastor of a local Christian Reformed Church, inviting me to attend a small prayer meeting in his office with a few other pastors. The intention was simply to pray for our city. Our city is widely known as a hard mission field, very liberal and secular, open to almost every spiritual expression. Conservative Christianity is the one option regarded with a special and peculiar disdain (one is that is regarded as "religious" and "institutional" instead of being fashionably "spiritual"). Our little gathering grew over a period of time, and soon we had perhaps twenty-five or thirty pastors in regular attendance.

We began to have monthly luncheons to which we would regularly invite some city, county or university official. At these meetings, we began asking these officials to describe their responsibilities and the needs that were "too big for any man or woman to help you with." We would then pray for these officials. To our amazement, almost all of these officials, liberal and secular in outlook, were very open to us praying for what were very difficult and even impossible situations. Even more to our amazement was when we began to see answers to our prayers, sometimes very direct and concrete. Let me give an example or two.[2]

We came to know several of the heads of the law enforcement agencies very well. In fact, one of the things we quickly learned was how much pastors and law enforcement officers have in common. Both are in contact with people in what are sometimes situations of desperation and both deal with people at the most extreme level of need. One police officer said to me, "We both deal with human depravity all the time—just from different angles."

The first time one of the heads of one of these agencies came to speak to us, we asked him at the end of his presentation how we could pray for him. "If we could pray for something that is too big for any man or woman to help you with, what would that be?" He thought for a few moments and then said that a university football game was coming up that was between the two great conference rivals, and things often got out of hand. There were always fights, and even riots. "I would like you to pray for peace on that night and over the weekend." So we did, right there, and promised to keep praying. We then told him we would check in with him after that weekend and get a report. The weekend came and went, and somebody saw him and asked what happened. "It was damn boring," he said. "Somebody pushed somebody in one of the taverns, and that was all

---

2 Part of my own inspiration for boldly praying for officials came from the examples I read about in the South American Pentecostal evangelist, Ed Silvoso, chronicled n his book *That None Should Perish,* Regal Books, Ventura, California 1994. I would also recommend *Taking Our Cities For God,* by John Dawson Creation House, Lake Mary, Florida 1989 Charismatics have done some excellent thinking on this matter.

that happened all weekend." It opened the door a little more and created more trust. God really did seem to answer our prayer. What happened was out of the realm of the ordinary.

On another occasion, we invited a newly elected county official to speak to us. I was the person who issued the invitation and I talked to her personally. "When you come, think about something related to your office that is too big for any man or woman to help you with, and we will pray for it." When she came, we had our lunch, introduced her as our guest and speaker, and she spoke for fifteen or twenty minutes about her responsibilities and what her office did. At the end, I asked her about something for us to pray for. She had not only thought about it, and not only had a request; she had a whole list that she brought with her. She told us what they were, and I wrote the list out on a white board that was in the room. And then, we sat her in a chair, surrounded her, laid hands on her and proceeded to pray for all of those items. She wanted to see us again, and she did in a few months. Every one of the requests was answered. I no longer remember what any of them were, except the last one, which was a request for someone who was "tall, dark, and handsome." She wanted to marry again. Indeed, he came along, and they were married in a church wedding. They returned to the church of her childhood, and for sometime thereafter, became weekly dinner guests of the priest who married them, and they discussed the church's doctrine of social theory.

In these situations I began to take the role of point man, following up with these officials. A number of these people became friends, and for some I became a pastor. Some became Christians, and many of them had a new openness to Christianity and Jesus Christ. In many cases (maybe most), they had virtually no non-politicized relationships that were "safe" where they could discuss various difficulties associated with their office and responsibilities. I became that one "safe person" they knew, although in truth, I might indeed have been very "unsafe" in spiritual ways.

Over a period of years, the programmatic side of our ministerial association waned, and perhaps its natural life span ended. Several pastors indicated that they longed for smaller gatherings in which to develop relationships with other pastors. Our gatherings with officials more or less came to an end, but my role as pastor to many of these officials and my role as a connector of pastors did not end. I came to be viewed as something of an unofficial bishop who was broadly in touch with a great many people in the city, both ecclesiastically and officially, as a pastor and counselor.

FRIENDSHIP AND PASTORING

One of the relevant factors in my ministry to public officials is that in my pastoral career I was the pastor of a very small church. The church I pastored never reached more than a hundred. In my experience, there is a built in bias in any search for city elders to concentrate on the pastors of the largest and most "wealthy" churches. It is commonly assumed that these pastors are pastors who have influence and know how to get things done. But what became clear was that, more often than not, a pastor of a large church would not be the best suited for this sort of ministry.

In the first place, large church pastors are often not pastors at all. They tend to be, in Peter Wagner's word, ranchers.[3] They are good at managing large staffs, and, if they are successful, they are good delegators. They are often the same kind of people who become civic leaders.

Some instances are clearly suited to ranchers. In our city, the mobilization of churches for volunteer labor for the school systems on one weekend a year and for other outreaches to the city is definitely the purview of ranchers. There are many areas where the competence, gifts and abilities of executive pastors of large churches are the most the perfect fit. But this is not true everywhere.

There is a division of labor, and part of what is needed is intensely personal one-on-one pastoral work. This means that pastors who are gifted to lead small churches may actually be better at doing this work. What is needed is not someone who is an impressive leader or administrator, but someone with a deep capacity for friendship and individual care.[4]

It is also the case that if a pastor comes from a small church there is no rivalry for a leader to fear. Pastors of large churches don't impress civic leaders, rather they are likely to be viewed as competition, in charge of large bodies of people who constitute voting blocks and pressure groups.

There is in this kind of ministry real opportunity for different leaders than we are accustomed to. Much of this is a ministry of one on one friendship. One official told me that he found my visits "very therapeutic" and that outside of his brother-in-law he had no one else he could discuss most of the problems he revealed to me, and, even with his

---

3 *Your Spiritual Gifts Can Help Your Church Grow*, Wagner, C. P. (1994), Ventura, Calif., Regal Books. pp.162-163

4 One of my elders in trying to offer constructive criticism to me to help improve my leadership style, said to me once, "Rich, you can't be everybody's best friend." What he said pointed to both a strength and a weakness in me.

brother-in-law, he had to be careful. I learned how lonely and isolated many officials are. For many or even most of them, the only reason they are approached is because people are angry with them or because they want something from them. Hardly anyone thinks of them as human beings who have very limited resources and real needs.

ANALOGIES OF PASTORING TO CIVIC LEADERSHIP

One of the analogies I discovered was that being the pastor of a church (even a small church) has many parallels to being a civic leader. I once ministered to the president of one of the great institutions in our city. She and I more than once observed that being the pastor of even a small church, in interesting and relevant ways, is similar to being in charge of a billion dollar enterprise like she was. There are obvious differences, but what is the same is that a pastor of a church is a lightening rod for conflict, just as she was. A pastor faces the same frequent sabotage and the same array of triangulation and human dysfunction. The human equation is very similar, however different the institutions are in both mission and size.

These same analogies are not quite as relevant for a pastor seeking to address the business world as for government and non-profit institutions. Profit entities ultimately function around the bottom-line of making money, and the profit/loss line gives a kind of orientation that does not exist in churches, universities, schools, non-profits and government agencies and entities. Orientation in all of those institutions is far more elusive, far more difficult to reckon with wisely. In a for-profit enterprise, if one is making widgets, the success or failure of that enterprise can be tracked with a profit and loss ledger. However, in a non-profit enterprise, tracking one's success or failure is far more difficult and intangible. Educating college students or helping the homeless to find permanent housing may be the goal, but tracking the success or failure in that mission is not so easy to track or define.[5] What do you mean by "educated," or what counts as "success" in helping the homeless, who rarely begin again to function like middle class counterparts? "Making a profit" is easier to define and understand than more intangible and elusive concepts like "being educated," "healthy," "stable."

No institution on earth is as complex as the Church. It is more similar to the civic and non-profit organization than for-profit entities, but neither one has the fullness of human relations, configurations and potential conflicts that the Church does.[6]

EVIL

The Church is the special target of demonic attack. The Church is the bull's-eye for evil and satanic forces. The Apostle Paul warned the Ephesian elders about antagonists, people who are inwardly ravenous and seek positions of influence and authority. "For I know this, that after my

---

5 James Collins, the author of *Good to Great,* has thought about this a great deal, and has written what amounts to an addendum to the above book dealing with for profit corporations that deals specifically with this issue for non-profits. (*Good to Great and the Social Sectors: A Monograph to Accompany Good to Great,* Jim Collins; 2005)

6 Edwin Friedman's classic *Generation to Generation,* makes this point repeatedly. Churches and Synagogues are multigenerational configurations of families that all transcend family and become a spiritual institution.
Friedman, E. H. (1985). *Generation to generation : family process in church and synagogue.* New York, Guilford Press. p.5-6, 162-190

departure savage wolves will come in among you, not sparing the flock. Also from among yourselves men will rise up, speaking perverse things, to draw away disciples after themselves." (Acts 20:29-30) The culmination of Jesus' ministry was in conflict with perverse religious authorities. He gives extended warnings about certain character types and failings in Matthew 23. Scott Peck, in *People of the Lie*, outlines five characteristics of evil people that are, interestingly, the same characteristics that Jesus condemns in this passage. They are:

1. Persistent scapegoating (Matt. 23:31-36) p.73

2. The seeking of extraordinary authority over others (Matt. 23: 2, 6, 7) p.177

3. Caring particularly about outward appearances (Matt. 23:5) p.75

4. Blindness to internal moral corruption and a self image of righteousness (Jesus repeatedly calls them "blind guides") (Matt. 23:16, 17, 24, 26) p.72

5. Extraordinary willfulness and an unsubmitted will (Matt. 23:15) p.77-84[7]

What particularly qualifies a pastor to function as a counselor to those in positions of authority is that, if he has been faithful in his calling, he will have had to learn how to deal with evil and antagonists.

I discovered repeatedly that leaders are troubled by antagonists and divisive people,[8] but they do not even have

---

7 Peck, M. S. (1983). *People of the Lie : the Hope for Healing Human Evil*. New York, Simon and Schuster.

8 For example, Paul instructs Timothy about this kind of person in I Timothy 6:4-5. "…he is conceited and understands nothing. He has an unhealthy interest in controversies and quarrels about words that result in envy, strife, malicious talk, evil suspicions, and constant friction between men of corrupt mind, who have been robbed of the truth…." (NIV) The entire epistles of II Peter and Jude are devoted to dealing with this kind of troubler, who was apparently a common figure in the 1st century church.

a vocabulary for them. Not only is the secular powerless before evil, but it is often officially committed to the denial of its reality. This makes institutions sitting ducks for take over artists. Virtually every official I have dealt with is up against this sort of evil, and it is not just those in law enforcement, although they do encounter it in its rawest and criminal forms. All institutions deal with this more subtly, sometimes in their own staff, and sometimes in the people they serve, but all of these officials need someone they can talk to and trust. Most of them have no one who has expertise and authority in these realities, and it is not even named, let alone dealt with.

DEATH AND RESURRECTION

The death and resurrection of Christ is now the central and final fact of the world, and it was the decisive blow to evil. I am going to argue that it is also the central reality of leadership. The theory of leadership presented in this book is a theory of martyrdom. One must experience a type of death before one can be raised to new life and authority to deal with evil and problems that are otherwise intractable.

There is nothing new in this. The Church Calendar, which is used by all liturgical communions (Catholics, Orthodox, Lutherans, Episcopalians), remembers a saint for every day of the year, and it remembers them not on their birthday (other than Jesus on Christmas and a handful of other figures), but on the day of their martyrdom or of their death (the day of their exodus to Heaven). The ancient and pagan world was conquered by martyrs. Can modernity be re-Christianized by anything else?

He has never stopped being a common figure, and he makes regular appearances today.

Islam is the perverse mirror image of Christendom,[9] and it is today attacking the West by the power of false martyrdom. Is it not necessary to re-understand the power of martyrdom in Jesus Christ? Even if full martyrdom is not called for, a real encounter with death still is called for.[10] David only became a great king, for example, because of his years in the wilderness fleeing Saul, and this constituted a kind of death. Paul overcame the Roman Empire from whipping posts and prisons. In today's world, authority still comes by means of wildernesses and what seem like whipping posts and imprisonments. We are called to have "eyes to see," so what may be typically viewed as hazards to be avoided, or hardships to be resented, may instead be seen as paths to transformation.

On a very large scale in the modern world, leadership by martyrdom can be seen in the extraordinary downfall of Communism at the end of the 20th Century. In the triumvirate of Margaret Thatcher, Ronald Reagan, and John Paul II, Reagan and John Paul both had narrow escapes from death when both nearly died at the hands of assassins. Both of them believed they were spared by God for the mission of toppling Communism. Reagan, who had always had a belief in predestination, had a great deepening in his faith that God's hand was in all things and especially

---

9 Leithart, P. (2007). "Mirror of Christendom: Why Islam Exists and What To Do About It." *Views and Reviews: Open Book Occasional Papers* 24: 15.

10 John Collins states that every "Level Five" leader that he and his team encountered, were marked by peculiar humility combined with extraordinary power of will, and many had either experienced a religious conversion or had come close to death and come back from that experience.
Collins, J. C. (2001). Good to great: why some companies make the leap--and others don't. New York, NY, Harper Business. pp. 17-40

in this.[11] It is doubtful that either man would have had the authority or wisdom to do what they did had they not come back from the dead.[12]

THE ADVISOR TO THE KING GOES FIRST

The advisor is likewise called to experience death and resurrection. If he or she does not, they will lack the requisite authority to help the leader they are dealing with.

---

11 Kengor, P. (2004). God and Ronald Reagan: A Spiritual Life. New York, Regan Books pp. 197-216

12 It has become the minority report that Thatcher, Reagan, and John Paul were the real force behind the collapse of Communism, and it is now commonly said that the entire event was somehow "inevitable" and would have happened no matter what. But it is very odd that during that era, Reagan alone was predicting the collapse of Communism, and the people now declaring the "inevitability" of its collapse, laughed at his bumpkin notions, and declared that Communism "was here to stay" and that it had now been amply proven that the Soviet style command economy had produced "remarkable results" fully the equal of the West.

D'Souza, D. (1997). Ronald Reagan : how an ordinary man became an extraordinary leader. New York, Free Press. Chapter 1, "The Wise Men and the Dummy"

Anthony Sutton demonstrated that Communism, because of its economically self destructive nature, was repeatedly on the verge of collapse through the early to middle twentieth century. It was however, repeatedly propped up by the West, and not allowed to collapse. Sutton, A. C. (1968). Western technology and Soviet economic development. Stanford, Calif., Hoover Institution on War Revolution and Peace Stanford University.

Thatcher, Reagan, and John Paul pushed the tottering giant to the cliff's edge and did nothing to stop it when it began tumbling. It was also the case that the combined rhetoric of these leaders disestablished any vestige of moral respectability left behind the Iron Curtain. Mikel Gorbochev certainly did his part. He appeared to want the demise of his own empire. He seems to have begun to believe in something else. Reagan on several occasions told his advisors that he suspected Gorbechev to be "a secret believer." He was right. Gorbechev made his faith public in 2008 when he made a pilgrimage to the tomb of Saint Francis of Assisi.

The two great biblical models for advisors to the king are Joseph and Daniel. Both experienced death and resurrection in their lives.

Joseph was sold into slavery by his brothers and taken to a foreign land. That was a death. He was then imprisoned because of his virtue while faithfully serving his foreign master. He was eventually raised from the dead by being called out of prison as an interpreter of nightmares and then appointed the Prime Minister of the entire nation. He finally revealed himself to his brothers in Genesis 45 ("'I am Joseph; does my father still live?' But his brothers could not answer him, for they were dismayed in his presence….'I am Joseph your brother whom you sold into Egypt.'" Genesis 45:3-4) This is one of the first typological foreshadowings of the Resurrection of Christ in the Bible.

Daniel likewise was a refugee. He also faced death when he was put into the lion's den. His three associates and friends, Shadrach, Meshach and Aben-Nego, were likewise thrown into the fiery furnace. In both cases, there was an emergence in a resurrection.

The advisor must pass through great trial, grief, sorrow and difficulty or he will be unequipped to give the requisite help. Much of his calling is to enable the leader to pass through crisis, and sometimes crisis of great magnitude. What but the power of the Cross of Christ could possibly give someone the necessary strength and power to successfully pass through such deep waters?[13]

---

13 This calls to mind this amusing passage from G.K. Chesterton's great novel, *The Man Who Was Thursday*. Garbiel Syme volunteers to become a philosophical policeman in the battle against world-wide anarchism, and he meets Sunday in a completely dark room, and the following conversation ensues when he is recruited for his new position :
Somewhat dazed and considerably excited, Syme allowed himself to be led to a side-door in the long row of buildings of Scotland Yard. Almost before he knew what he was doing, he had been passed through the

A PARTICULAR ACCOUNT

A friend of mine gave a personal account that conveys the heart of this conviction. In an early pastorate, he came to a place of complete deadlock with his church. In all too typical fashion, he became the lightening rod for all of the problems in the church. He was blamed for everything and was repeatedly attacked and lied about. In one horrific congregational meeting, he was personally attacked and vilified and accused of numerous things that were clearly untrue. He described going home, putting his head in his wife's lap, and weeping like a baby. This went on for hours. He finally felt as though he had come to the complete end of himself. Astonishingly, he believed that it was God's will for him to stay and not to resign.

The next day, he went to his elders and said that he was determined to stay and that he would not leave. They were stunned. My friend was a dead man. He had been murdered the night before. And yet, here he was, alive and refusing to

---

hands of about four intermediate officials, and was suddenly shown into a room, the abrupt blackness of which startled him like a blaze of light. It was not the ordinary darkness, in which forms can be faintly traced; it was like going suddenly stone-blind.

"Are you the new recruit?" asked a heavy voice.

And in some strange way, though there was not the shadow of a shape in the gloom, Syme knew two things: first, that it came from a man of massive stature; and second, that the man had his back to him.

"Are you the new recruit?" said the invisible chief, who seemed to have heard all about it. "All right. You are engaged."

Syme, quite swept off his feet, made a feeble fight against this irrevocable phrase.

"I really have no experience," he began.

"No one has any experience," said the other, "of the Battle of Armageddon."

"But I am really unfit——"

"You are willing, that is enough," said the unknown.

"Well, really," said Syme, "I don't know any profession of which mere willingness is the final test." "I do," said the other—"martyrs. I am condemning you to death. Good day."

leave his post. What does one say to a dead man come back to life? They were speechless. That was the turning point. From that time on, he had the authority and wisdom to deal with that church's failings and needs. The church changed and prospered.[14]

Only a leader who comes back from the dead has the power to do this. And likewise, if one is called to be a counselor to leaders who will themselves have to experience this, then the counselor must likewise go through the same fires in some way before that can be a reality.

---

14 The accuracyof this account, and permission to use it, was confirmed to the writer in an e-mail from Rev. Williams on February 28, 2009.

Chapter Two

WHAT THE COUNSELOR TO THE KING MUST KNOW THAT THE KING DOES NOT KNOW

Both Joseph and Daniel had knowledge that neither the king nor his own in-house counselors had. Both of them had access to the light and wisdom of Heaven and therefore were able to understand secrets that otherwise were hidden and inaccessible to both the king and his court. It was this superior knowledge that gave them access eventually to the king's ear. Little has changed since then. It is still the case that God's servants know things that are unknown outside of God's kingdom and are capable of acting as interpreters to what is hidden and inaccessible to the world. As a counselor to the king a pastor can understand what is unknown to court counselors and thereby gain the attention of the king (I Corinthians 2:6-16, Ephesians 5:13-14). Only a Christian is capable of truly understanding and exposing the principle repression of our time and exposing the schizophrenic confusion that issues from it.

THE FOUNDATION OF MODERN CONFUSION AND LACK OF ORIENTATION:

THE DOCTOR AND HIS PATIENT: THE REPRESSED CONFLICT

A pastor may not have enough deep historical knowledge and experience to speak to the king, but he does have a large backlog of pastoral experience with individuals. If one gives intense attention to small things, it is possible to understand very large things. The individual human psyche in the modern and post-modern world bears within itself the entire scope of the vast historical and social panorama that is around him. He has absorbed it and he expresses it as a microcosm of the macrocosm. The micro and the macro give mutual expression in one another.

One can see this in past eras. Martin Luther, for example, carried within himself all of the dilemmas and contradictions of the late medieval period. Luther was the late medieval era, all in himself. When he found the key to his own dilemmas, he discovered, much to his own surprise, the key to the dilemmas of his own time, and the Protestant Reformation was born. A pastor dealing day in and day out with troubled souls in his own congregation has a window on the age. He sees in them in small print what is written large in the entire era.

The Apostle Paul develops his biblical theology in an analogous way when he traces Israel's development through the Old Testament to the coming of Christ. The Apostle presents the human race as a single human being who develops from a child to an adult (Galatians 4:1-7). In the time of the Law, the race was like a minor, or a slave, under the control of certain masters, teachers and tutors. But now, with the coming of Christ, the race has come into the time of the adult. Likewise, Paul says in Ephesians that we, in the Church of Christ, are to come to be "a perfect man, to the measure of the stature of the fullness of Christ, that we should no longer be children...." (Ephesians 4:11-16). It is as if Jesus was the world's first grown-up and now we are to follow in His maturity. This is a continuation of a theme we find in the book of Ezekiel. Through the prophet, God excoriates Israel who was originally found by God as an infant (in the time of the Egyptian slave captivity), which He saved when she was like an abandoned child. Now she has reached the age when she is nubile and, instead of joyously looking forward to marriage to Jehovah, she has become a whore, whoring after the gods of the nations (Ezekiel 16). The operative point here is that Israel is viewed as an individual, initially as a child, and then matures into young adulthood. Paul continued this theme by indicating that with the coming of Jesus Christ (Who represents all of Israel) we have seen adulthood for the first time. And now the Church is to follow and grow to the same stature as Jesus Christ Himself.

Dr. Paul Tournier unraveled the dilemma of our age through his counseling practice and was able to extrapolate it to an historical scale. In the same way if a pastor can understand the repressions and conflicts of his congregants, he can understand his age, and this provides an essential orientation for becoming an advisor to the king.

Dr. Paul Tournier was a Swiss physician in the twentieth century who, through his counseling work with his many patients, drew fascinating and telling analyses of modernity. In his book, *The Whole Person In a Broken World*, Tournier gives an analogical replication of the Apostle Paul's observations in seeing western man developing from the child in the medieval period, through adolescence at the time of the Renaissance, to a late and arrested adolescence in the present period. An arrested adolescence is the stage that we have now reached, and it is a stage characterized by Tournier as neurosis.

Tournier then asks, "...why do we say [this is a] neurosis and not simply a normal crisis of adolescence?"[15]

In answer, Tournier says there are three recognizable elements to neurosis: Anxiety, Sterility, and the presence of an Unconscious Conflict.[16] In his analysis this is a description of the whole modern situation.

Anxiety is a result of deep, hidden, inner dissatisfaction and conflict. In order to deal with this conflict, the modern man "poses both as an innocent man and as an accuser...." But under a flood of criticisms he conceals an inner anxiety.[17]

This inner anxiety leads to sterility of action. "What is more, the tragic thing about neurotics is that the very efforts they make to save themselves destroy them." Tournier goes on to say, "I find the same paradox in the modern world. The efforts it makes to save itself bring it to ruin. The efforts it makes to avert war pitch it into war. The efforts it makes to guarantee its material security disrupt the economy and increase its misery. The efforts it makes to penetrate the secrets of nature and capture its energy lead to the atomic bomb, which threatens to destroy everything it has built up in the course of the centuries. The efforts it makes to

---

15 Tournier, P. (1964). *The Whole Person in a Broken World*. New York, Harper & Row. p. 8

16 Ibid. p. 8-10

17 Ibid. p. 8

free man from social slavery plunge it into struggles which only increase his burdens.... This behavior which produces the opposite of what is desired is one of the specific characteristics of neurosis, giving it the appearance of a curse, a doom, a rushing into self destruction, a demonic force."[18]

And the neurotic is characterized by an unconscious conflict. With the coming of the Renaissance, "humanity rejected that which it had hitherto allowed to guide it. It resolved to pay no more attention to any judgment of value, no longer to trust any metaphysical intuition, any poetic inspiration, any supernatural revelation, and to build its civilization solely upon material realities and objective knowledge." Tournier then bridges the gap between what began in the Renaissance and what has evolved to full bloom neurosis in the modern era. He gives this definition that all too often characterizes our time. "A person is a neurotic when he has repressed something without having really eliminated it. Modern man thinks he has eliminated the world of values, the world of poetry, the world of moral consciousness, but he has only repressed it and is suffering from it."[19]

Tournier gives a particular case history of a single patient, a young man named Max, who is in conflict with his father. He is failing in school and spends all of his time listening to jazz in various clubs. His father is an authority who represents the entire world of adulthood and responsibility, and yet Max has seen egregious moral failings and hypocrisies in his father, especially in relation to his mother that have caused Max to rebel. And yet Max is ambivalent in this relationship and cannot bring himself

18 Ibid. p. 9

19 Ibid. p. 10-11

to completely reject and hate his father and all that he stands for. He is, in fact, aware of own moral failings and weaknesses for which he likewise has no solution, and his rebellion is at bottom a running away from himself.

I am often asked what I think of the relations between sin and sickness. The following outline seems to me to give a clear picture of it:

> The son who loves his father is right and healthy. The son who hates his father is not right, but healthy. The son who loves and hates his father at the same time is neurotic.
>
> Neurosis rests upon an inner contradiction and this is what makes it possible for many doctors to say that the neurotic son will be cured if he frees himself from his moral scruples and hates his father with all his heart. Other doctors, however, say that he will never be able to stifle completely his love and can only be cured by abandoning his hatred.
>
> In the same way, I believe that if humanity, since the Renaissance, had really been able to eliminate the spiritual, to "kill God," as some have believed it has, it would probably be less sick than it is today. I am not saying that it would be in the truth and in righteousness, but it would not be divided in soul; it would not be ambivalent.
>
> The collective man, of whom Pascal wrote, has rejected his childhood. He has rejected the moral criteria of the past and refused to recognize anything except the reason, the yardstick, and the scales. But the idea of the beautiful, the good, the just, his need for communion with his Creator, he has only been able to repress below the field of consciousness.
>
> Disgusted by the abuses to which it led, humanity repressed Christianity by which it had so long been dominated. Repressed, but not eliminated, Herein lies, I believe, the essence of the tragedy of modern times. The modern man lives as if Christianity were a negligible

> hypothesis with no relation to the concrete realities of
> the world and society. And yet at the bottom of his heart
> this man remains impregnated with Christianity so that
> he lives in a state of perpetual ambivalence with regard
> to it.[20]

Tournier quotes a certain Dr Stocker,[21] "Dr. Stocker has given us this penetrating definition of neurosis: an inner conflict between a false suggestion and a true intuition. A false suggestion from the modern world and a true intuition of the soul, which in reality yearns for something altogether different from science, power, and material goods…. Modern man suffers from repression of conscience."[22]

Tournier's book was published originally in French in 1947 and translated into English in 1964. One might argue that his thesis is somewhat shopworn now that post modernism is frontally attacking many of the conflicts of modernity that he was addressing. I would argue that rather post modernism has joined ranks with Dr. Tournier, but is itself far from bringing any resolution to modern neurosis. It rather exposed it, but without Dr. Tournier's cure of faith in Jesus Christ. It may be a further and even more convoluted repression of conscience.

This repression of conscience, which comes from the repression of Christianity, is more fundamental than any other repression of our time. Our patient is schizophrenic in his outlook and life. He longs for all of the values and

---

20 Ibid. pp.12-13, 16

21 Stocker, D. A. (1945). *Le Traitement moral des nerveux.* Geneva, Editions du Rhone.

22 Tournier, P. (1964). *The whole person in a broken world.* New York, Harper & Row. p. 12

realities of the Kingdom of God and at the same time is alienated from them, but he is unaware of this split and is therefore anxiety-ridden.

In sum, if the pastor understands this, he is in a position to understand the most crucial elements of our age. He is in a position to help people in public service because people in public service are amongst the most schizophrenic people of our time. Most of them are in public service precisely because of the values they have inherited from the Kingdom of God, but at the same time most of them are unaware of this or do not know where to go to become completed, unified and authentic. It is impossible in the long run to separate the second table of the Law from the first table.[23] Initially, most people in public service are there because in youthful idealism they wanted "to change the world" and "make the world a better place." These very ideals are for them relics inherited from the Christian Church. The very phrase, "I want to change the world," was the motive-phrase behind the missionary movement that dominated the Western church from the 18th through the 20th Centuries. What happens when you want to change the world, but have no divine power or commission behind you, and have forgotten that those missionaries who went off to change the world sometimes took their own coffins with them, expecting martyrdom, suffering and death? A pastor who understands this can be used to transform inherited relics into living spiritual weapons. The problem with our world is not just that at the deepest level that it is re-paganizing (it is), but that it is still half Christian and therefore lives in repression and frustration. Our re-paganization can never

---

23 The Ten Commandments. The so called "first table" are commandments about our relationship with God, and the second have reference to our obligation to our neighbor.

again become what it was in the ancient world. It must now always shape itself around a rejected and/or repressed Christianity. That is precisely what anti-Christ is. Anti-Christ must shape himself to look like Christ. And the only way to overcome a fraudulent anti-Christ is to know who the real One is and how He functions.

To learn how to deal with this, let's go to school for a while and examine this deep repression and schizophrenia in some detail. We need to know what it is so we can know how to deal with it. Gird up your loins and let's wade in.

OUR CURRENT SITUATION AND THE HISTORICAL BACKGROUND THAT LED TO IT

All of the issues that have led to the repression of Christianity are hidden in our past. The way we have organized our world, the way we have organized both civic and church life are outgrowths of and accommodations to this fundamental repression. And it is not just repressed on the individual level, but also socially and institutionally repressed.

National denominations have been the primary means of organizing and governing the Church since the Reformation and post-Reformation era. Denominations are a part of the nation-state Enlightenment solution that followed the Wars of Religion. They are a part and parcel of both an Enlightenment epistemology and political structure.

Denominations are configurations that allow many churches to peacefully co-exist in one geographical area with one political structure without any one of them dominating or attempting to dominate all others. This settlement has advantages and has given us both political and religious stability for several centuries, but it is also an imperfect settlement that has unresolved tensions within it that are now surfacing in serious fashion such that the Enlightenment solution has become questionable.

Luther proved, despite his wishes, to be a Samson who at the end of his life had one hand placed on the pillar of the state and one on the pillar of the Church. With gigantic strength, he toppled the orderly temple that had given unity and structure to the world for ten centuries. As Germanic princes broke free from the control of both the Emperor and the Pope, the right of the prince to establish the church of his own choice emerged as a revolutionary right. The Thirty Years War ensued. These so called Wars of Religion reflected the resistance of the old order against relinquishing its ancient hold that dates back to Constantine. The right of the Papacy to exercise supreme religious authority over all kings and the emperor was effectively over.[24]

RESOLUTION TO RELIGIOUS WAR

On September 25, 1555, the ink began drying on the fresh signing of the Peace of Augsburg, and, in a definable way, a new era was begun. The seed of the secular state

---

24 Shelley, B. L. (1982). *Church history in plain language*. Dallas, Word Pub. p. 322. Christianity had already obviated many of the ancient pagan unifications of the state and religion from the very beginning. Separation of church and state was not an innovation of the post-Reformation world, but was introduced from the beginning of Christianity's influence on the state. The battle between pope and emperor was an ancient and ongoing battle, and the rights of the king were different than the rights of the priest. This differentiation from paganism in which the state was often a cathedral state, in which the temple was a department of state, and in which the king or pharaoh was himself a god, was all overthrown by Christianity. The post-Reformation world simply carried elements of the genius of Christianity further forward. It did not introduce them for the first time. Rushdoony, R. J. (1971). *The one and the many; studies in the philosophy of order and ultimacy*. [Nutley, N.J.], Craig Press. pp. 124-184

that could be defined around an axis of not one church, not the only true church, not the Church of Rome, but the church chosen by the prince of that palatine was launched. Ninety-three years later, the Treaty of Westphalia (May 25th and October 24th, 1648) took the unprecedented step of allowing for more than one church to co-exist in a palatine at the same time, if the prince so chose. It was possible for subjects to now choose whether to be Lutheran, Calvinist or even Catholic, with no interference from the Papacy. "After more than a thousand years, the state was free to transact its business as though the Pope did not exist."[25]

In this there were great advances and the new found liberty unleashed great creativity, but no settlement in this world is final, and, as always, unintended consequences were introduced along with the advances. Today we are still trying to come to grips with these problems.

Denominationalism is how the Church came to cope with what followed religious war and represents both a successful settlement of the religious question and a corollary to other inherent problems inside the modern church.[26]

The Wars of Religion were the result of the dogma that the obligation of the prince (or more generically, the state) was to uphold the Truth and Dogma and the true Church.[27] Along side this, the state had its foundation in the decree of God that was testified to by the Church as it read the Scriptures.

---

25 Page 322, *Church History in Plain Language*, Bruce Shelley

26 Shelley, B. L. (1982). *Church history in plain language*. Dallas, Word Pub. pp. 319-326

27 Ibid. pp. 320-322

The first major split in the Church occurred long before the Reformation.[28] The split with the East and Byzantine had happened centuries before, but, in spite of pressures and tensions, the Western church had managed to maintain a fundamental unity until the time of Luther. With the Reformation, the long standing feud between Pope and King was heightened and, eventually, the tenuous connection was severed in Protestant Europe and effectively severed in areas that remained Catholic. The prince, or the state, however, continued to uphold the dogma that the religious affiliation of the populace (which was not a choice on their part) was an obligation of obedience to the prince in his discernment and choice. However, after Westphalia, the possibility of free thought and free choice on the part of families and even individuals was now a new horizon that could not be repressed. When the Treaty of Augsburg was concluded, it allowed each prince to determine which church, Lutheran or Catholic, would be the official church of that palatine. But beyond that Westphalia opened the possibility of several churches co-existing within the same boundaries including beyond the Lutheran, the Catholic, the Calvinist churches. Anabaptist groups were still anathema, but after Westphalia complete freedom of families and even individuals to exercise religious freedom were impossible to repress.[29]

---

28 The Eastern and Western Church reached a final fissure in 1054 that is still with us to this day. And earlier there had been significant splits with the Nestorian churches which are still with us as well.

González, J. L. (1996). *Church history : an essential guide.* Nashville, Abingdon Press. pp. 13-15, 46-49

29 Shelley, B. L. (1982). *Church history in plain language.* Dallas, Word Pub. p. 320-322

González, J. L. (1996). *Church history : an essential guide.* Nashville, Abingdon Press. p.77

The corollary to allowing freedom of religion was a transformation of the understanding of long traditional relationship of the King and Prince to the Church and religion. The Enlightenment solution transformed public understanding of truth. In the Middle Ages, truth was a theological concept; it was settled and arbitrated by the Church. After the Wars of Religion it appeared to be impossible to ever again have a settled and public agreement concerning theological truth. The Church previously settled truth, but now the Church was rent apart into several warring factions, and truth could never be agreed upon in a seamless public way. Hence, there was an entire paradigm shift.[30] Theology was placed in the realm of opinion and became increasingly a private and personal affair, and empirically testable theses were placed in the realm of truth. The state from now on was to be based, not on theology, but on certain self evident truths that were founded on a natural law that was not tied to any particular ecclesiastical institution or revealed religion.

While certain truths were deemed self-evident, western man was not yet able to declare himself transparently autonomous and godless. A metaphysical and

---

30 This is an apt example of a sociological application of Kuhn's thesis concerning science in his *The Structure of Scientific Revolutions*. "Normal science" functions at most times, and problems or anomalies are dealt with and absorbed within a particular paradigm. But at a certain point, the anomalies are so numerous, and so severe, that the paradigm can no longer absorb or adjust to them, and an entirely new paradigm is necessary. The collapse of medieval political theology, as a paradigm is almost strictly analogous.

Kuhn, T. S. (1962). *The structure of scientific revolutions*. Chicago [Ill.], University of Chicago Press.

An example of an application of models and paradigms to various contexts in theology is found in Bevans, S. B. (1992). *Models of contextual theology*. Maryknoll, N.Y., Orbis Books.

even theological foundation was still thought necessary. There is a line of descent that is observable in tracing the metaphysical foundation of public truth and statecraft. After the medieval settlement, the first devolution from Christian orthodoxy is to Deism, thus providing a minimal foundation in the divine for what is still a creation. But Deism was both an unstable and unnecessary foundation and eventually devolved to naturalism and consequently to positivism, instrumentalism, existentialism and finally post modernism.[31]

It is arguable that it is not possible to function without a divinity, but that humanity itself, and the state itself, became the new divinity in the form of vast new idols. In the most virulent forms in the 20th century, the divinized state took the form of Nazism and Communism, but it took milder forms in the western democracies.

In all of this, denominationalism became the accepted way of coping with the diverse theological opinions of various churches. Each denomination was to be given liberty to practice its own cultus, but it practiced at the cost of each church being confined to the realm of opinion and not considered the purveyor of public truth. The Church has ever since struggled with public irrelevance.

This situation and settlement has been the case, with relevant differences, in both Europe and America. In England, for example, there is still a state church, and the crowned head of state is still deemed the head of that church. However, the Free Church movement was very much a reality in Britain and in the rest of Europe. While

---

31 For a helpful and concise tracing of this devolution, one can consult, Sire, J. W. (1997). *The universe next door : a basic worldview catalog.* Downers Grove, Ill, InterVarsity Press.

there is still an established church with a royal head, the royal family have themselves been relegated to a non-essential sphere along with the Church. The Parliamentary rule functions in the realm of public truth with much the same Enlightenment understanding as other secular governments. In Britain both the Established Church and the Crown function with the paradox of being viewed as interesting and perhaps even essential institutions, but institutions that are anachronistic. This British schizophrenia is characteristic of the whole of the western world and represents the inherent and unsolved problem of the Enlightenment settlement. The Truth as it is found in the Bible and the Christian Church can never in its own self definition be relegated to opinion and the private realm.[32]

AN AMERICAN TEST CASE: RHODE ISLAND

The first secular state in the world was the state of Rhode Island,[33] though it was a footnote to its federal parent, the United States of America. Neither the Constitution of Rhode Island nor the Constitution of the United States permit a religious test requiring membership in any specific church body or denomination for office holders, and both make acknowledgement of Jesus Christ oblique

---

32 The 2nd and the 110th Psalms, for example, are extensively quoted by the Apostles in the New Testament (Acts 4:25-26, I Cor. 15:25, Eph. 1:22) as texts which point to the subjection of all principalities, powers, kings, and rulers to the Messiah, who is now ruling at the Right Hand of the Father as the King of Kings.

33 How a Very Religious Nation Produced the First Secular State. *The Twelve Tribes: the Commonwealth of Israel* Volume, DOI: http://www.twelvetribes.com/publications/roger-williams/roger-williams-intro.html
"Secular" does not mean "godless," but without ecclesiastical foundation or connection.

and indirect.[34] Neither state envisioned an atheistic state emerging at any point, but both also purposely embrace a non-ecclesiastical foundation for their authority.[35]

What was normative for every state, empire, monarchy and tribal configuration until the French Revolution was an explicitly visible religious foundation. Now in the new world this was overturned.

---

34 The term, "Year of Our Lord," in both documents *is* an oblique acknowledgement of Jesus Christ.

35 Ibid. *Volume*, DOI: Tavard, G. H. (1967). *The pilgrim church*. [New York], Herder and Herder.
    Preamble

We, the people of the State of Rhode Island and Providence. Plantations, grateful to Almighty God for the civil and religious liberty which He hath so long permitted us to enjoy, and looking to Him for a blessing upon our endeavors to secure and to transmit the same unimpaired to succeeding generations, do ordain and establish this Constitution of government. Declaration of Rights. Sec. 3.Whereas Almighty God hath created the mind free; and all attempts to influence it by temporal punishments or burdens, or by civil incapacitations, tend to beget habits of hypocrisy and meanness; and whereas a principal object of ourvenerable ancestors, in the migration to this country and their settlement of this state, was, as they expressed it,to hold forth a lively experiment that a flourishing civil state may stand and be best maintained with the full liberty in religious concernments: We, therefore, declare that no man shall be compelled to frequent or to support any religious worship, place, or ministry whatever, except in fulfillment of his own voluntary contract; nor enforced, restrained, molested, or burdened in his body or goods; nor disqualified from holding any office; nor otherwise suffer on account of his religious belief; and that every man shall be free to worship God according to the dictates of his own conscience, and to profess and by argument to maintain his opinion in matters of religion; and that the same shall in no wise diminish, enlarge, or effect his civil capacity.

School, C. U. L. United States Constitution Article VI. Volume, DOI: http://www.law.cornell.edu/constitution/constitution.articlevi.html
    Article VI

The Senators and Representatives before mentioned, and the members of the several state legislatures, and all executive and judicial officers, both of the United States and of the several states, shall be bound by oath or affirmation, to support this Constitution; but no religious test shall ever be required as a qualification to any office or public trust under the United States.

The Rhode Island settlement came very close to being a perfect expression of the modern dilemma of how the Church and State, the Kingdom of God and the Kingdom of the world, are to relate. On the one hand there is a clear desire to separate the two since power corrupts and power politics seem in many ways antithetical to the Kingdom of God. On the other hand, there is a desire for the state to be tamed and christianized. Anabaptist theology and churches want to live with Christian princes and governments every bit as much as the Magisterial Reformers did, but without resorting to any kind of power politics along the way. Rhode Island was essentially an Anabaptist Settlement in regard to the relationship of church and state, but it is questionable how stable a settlement it could be.

There has always been an Anabaptist perspective that sees the conversion of Constantine and the adoption of Christianity in the late Roman Empire as its official religion as the worst catastrophe that has ever come upon the Church.[36] Christians associated themselves with the state, and, unavoidably, the Church was sometimes, even frequently, corrupted. There is plenty of evidence that this is so, and these abuses and their human consequences are the data for much of the thesis of the rest of this book. There are, in fact, so many that the Anabaptist solution of complete sectarian withdrawal from the sphere of the state is tempting. But is this really possible or wise?

Roger Williams, the founder of Rhode Island, asserted among other things that "the civil power of the state could

---

36 Broadbent, E. H. (1931). *The pilgrim church, being some account of the continuance through succeeding centuries of churches practising the principles taught and exemplified in the New Testament.* London [etc.], Pickering & Inglis.
Neuhaus, R. J. (1984). *The naked public square : religion and democracy in America.* Grand Rapids, Mich., W.B. Eerdmans Pub. Co. p.172

properly have no jurisdiction over the consciences of men." He was the first and foremost American proponent of the theory of the absolute freedom of the individual in matters of religion.[37] But, if it be the case that the state can have no rule or say over the consciences of individuals in religious matters, is it also the case that the Church has no say over the consciences of those in the state over matters touching the political? And if the state can have no say over matters of religion, then is religion to be entirely confined to the sphere and realm of the private? Can religion not encroach on the realm of the public where it might come into conflict with the political sphere of the state?

The entire Constitution of Rhode Island is a little masterpiece of the exposition of human rights. It forbids the practice of slavery, the quartering of soldiers, double indemnity, and it protects the right to trial by jury, private property, the assumption of innocence and many other rights.[38] Where did these rights come from, and why should they be respected? It ought to be noted that the Constitution of Rhode Island itself recognizes in a number of places the existence and power of God and clearly sees God as the source of rights and human dignity. It clearly states that God is the source of liberty of conscience. In this case (as is the case with many documents coming from this era), the term "secular" oddly has a meaning that is still inside the jurisdiction and metaphysics of Christendom. This existence of the God of the Christians is actually a pre-theoretical presupposition that is all controlling. This entire

---

37 Williams, Roger. *Encyclopedia Britannica*. New York, The Encyclopedia Britannica Company. 28: 682-683.

38 The Constitution of the State of Rhode Island. Volume, DOI: http://www. harbornet.com/rights/r-island.txt

affair of a non-interfering state which upholds the rights of individual conscience only works on the assumption that the state is already Christian or Christianized. But the Rhode Island Constitution also divorced the Church, and implicitly any visible connection to the Kingdom of God, from the state. If this hidden background disappears, then one is left with naked human authority which no longer has any obligation to respect liberty of conscience. The Anabaptist convictions of the prevailing church then forbid interjecting themselves into the Realpolitik of statecraft. Such interjections would lead to a renewed Constantinian Settlement, which was anathema. This nakedly secular state (with no Christendom as a background) would have no obligation to respect the liberty of conscience of individual Christians or churches and could, in an untrammeled way, practice persecution and coercion.

One might make a case for the necessity of Anabaptists themselves living with the consequence of persecution, but to be consistent, such a church would also have to allow for the return of slavery for example (something Anabaptist groups would find especially abhorrent). Futhermore an unjust state does not just persecute the Church, but will finally extend unjust authority to every sphere. Does one then simply accept, in sectarian retreat, all of the consequences of a completely anti-Christian and beastly state? Or in the other direction, does one simply accept all of the consequences of unfettered liberty of conscience on the part of individuals? What if individuals, on religious grounds, decide to live in polygamy, or decide to open houses of prostitution, or sell recreational drugs in residential neighborhoods? What if unfettered pornography, abortion, unscrupulous money lending and homosexual hustling are the choices of one's pagan neighbors? On what grounds does the state interfere with such individual life style choices?

The United States, with its foundational documents of the Declaration of Independence and the Constitution, likewise appears to have a shell or canopy of an almost invisible Christendom over it. The United States as a federal government had no established denomination, but was made up of original states in which almost all of them did. Thus, America, through the states, was still very close to an established church. By 1833, however, the last established denomination (in Massachusetts) was disestablished.[39] This did not undo the Christian character of America, but merely re-invigorated it in a volunteeristic form.[40] The free church and volunteeristic form of the Kingdom of God have always been deeply tinctured in the nation's temperament. Tocqueville noted this very early in America's history.[41]

---

39 United States of America. *MSN Encarta Volume,* DOI: http://uk.encarta.msn. com/encyclopedia_761573010_3/United_States_of_America.html

40 Noll, M. (2007) America's Two Foundings. *First Things Volume,* DOI: http:// www.firstthings.com/article.php3?id_article=6082

41 See, e.g., Alexis de Tocqueville, Democracy in America (1835) (tr. Henry Reeves1899) vol. I, ch.17 (Principal Causes Maintaining The Democratic RepublicPart III) : In France I had almost always seen the spirit of religion and the spirit of freedom marching in opposite directions. But in America I found they were intimately united and that they reigned in common over the same country. My desire to discover the causes of this phenomenon increased from day to day. In order to satisfy it I questioned the members of all the different sects; I sought especially the society of the clergy, who are the depositaries of the different creeds and are especially interested in their duration. As a member of the Roman Catholic Church, I was more particularly brought into contact with several of its priests, with whom I became intimately acquainted. To each of these men I expressed my astonishment and explained my doubts. I found that they differed upon matters of detail alone, and that they all attributed the peaceful dominion of religion in their country mainly to the separation of church and state. I do not hesitate to affirm that during my stay in America I did not meet a single individual, of the clergy or the laity, who was not of the same opinion

Retreat from the sphere of the state on the part of the Church is not simple. Even if at the extremity one argues that one is obligated to live as a consistent pacifist and offer no resistance to the injustices of any state other than prayer and martyrdom, this approach could lead to a political consequence that would still press the question regarding the relationship between Church and state. After all, the early Church prayed and suffered martyrdom only to eventually see the prevailing pagan power structure crumble and undergo conversion. What does one do if and when the emperor is converted? Does one turn him away, or tell him his obligation is to abdicate his political responsibilities, or that his new found faith bears no relationship to his role as magistrate?

Today, we are living in a world where both unfettered and beastly states and unfettered anarchic individual liberty are at work everywhere. Rhode Island and the United States are not final resting places, but are places in a process that has now become very uncomfortable, contradictory and anomalous enough that a renewal of the relationship of Church and State, God's Kingdom and the Kingdom of the World, must be found. What was an unstable relationship in Rhode Island, and perhaps for a long time, a still rocky if not more satisfactory relationship in the United States as a whole, is now reaching the level where some quarters long for a complete divorce. And the Church has struggled for a long time with how to be more than a private entity.

---

on this point. (Available online at http://www.gutenberg.org/etext/815 .) See also James Bryce, *The American Commonwealth* (London : MacMillan & Co., 1888), vol. III, 483: So far from suffering from want of State support, religion seems in the United States to stand all the firmer because, standing alone, she is seen to stand by her own strength. Lord Bryce (1838-1922), a British jurist, historian, politician and diplomat, was ambassador to the United States from 1907 to 1913.

Beyond the United States to all of the western world, the modern secular state is reaching the edges of being intolerably self-contradictory, and its very survival in any form is realistically now in question. Likewise, the Church continues to struggle with escaping the privatized realm to which she has been consigned or has consigned herself.

THE FACT / VALUE DISTINCTION

Hence, the modern fact/value distinction has historical origin. By this, I mean the view that the realm of "objective," empirical reality is separate from the realm of beliefs, such as theology, and ethics. The first is capable of being "true" or "false," the second is only "opinion." It is a way of dealing with the repression of the unresolved and embarrassing public reality of the entry of the Kingdom of God into the world. Jesus Christ is not just the Emperor of private space, the space of opinion, but also of public space. He is the Emperor and origin of all truth. The Church was the institution immediately affected by it, but there is no institution that is not affected by this split and this repression[42] This repression has caused many of our leaders and all of our institutions to be afflicted with the same

---

42 There is a great deal of foment in the philosophical world in regard to the utter inadequacy of the "fact/value" distinction. My own Calvinistic background has produced the remarkable thinking of Cornelius Van Til and Herman Dooyeweerd. One could add Alvin Plantinga to the Calvinistic group as well. Lesslie Newbigin has written profoundly on this issue in all of his books, and he is dependent upon the lucid and profound thought of Michael Polanyi. One can also point to the Thomist revival in the Roman Catholic Church with thinkers like Gilson and Maritain. For that matter, G. K. Chesterton was saying all of these things, perhaps better than anyone, and before anyone, in the early twentieth century in his incomparable classics, *Orthodoxy* and *The Dumb Ox*. Chesterton, G. K. (1933). *St. Thomas Aquinas.* New York,, Sheed & Ward, inc. Chesterton, G. K. (2004). *Orthodoxy.* Mineola, N.Y., Dover Publications.

symptoms as Tournier discovered in his patients: anxiety and sterility. The source is this deeply hidden and repressed conflict concerning King Jesus. A pastor can know this, and this knowledge is the beginning of his work with leaders in the modern world.

Chapter Three

HOW THE BIBLE SPEAKS TO THE TIMES: BECOMING A COUNSELOR TO THE KING

If one is called to be a counselor to the king how does one initially go about capturing his ear, and how does one advise him in regard to the times and their meaning?

Hamlet mused on this and concluded that

"The play's the thing,
Wherein I'll catch the conscience of the king."[43]

He knew that the King had to find himself in the midst of a narrative, in the midst of a story of which he becomes a participant. Beyond causing the King to identify himself and be convicted as in Hamlet, he or she must identify their problem and perhaps the solution within a predictable narrative flow.

The Bible has large measures of narrative. Where in the narrative do we find ourselves, first as counselors, and then what does the inspired narrative itself tell us about capturing the conscience of the king?

---

43 *Hamlet*, Act II, scene ii, lines 633-634

SPIRITUAL WARFARE

In the biblical narrative, we find various figures becoming involved in differing kinds of spiritual warfare encounters that transpire in enemy territory. These comprise a substantial portion of the Bible in both Old and New Testament.

First come power contests. I have given some examples of initial power encounters with several officials when they saw the prayers of the pastors answered. These capture attention and demonstrate that the God of the Bible is more powerful than any of the prevailing gods or of any of the principalities and powers. The account of Moses is the great power contest of the Old Testament. Jehovah, through His servant Moses, enters into contests of power with the gods of Egypt and finally completely vanquishes them (Exodus 3-15). One of the other notable Old Testament power contests is the contest of Elijah with the priests of Baal. That narrative also ends with the vanquishing of the foreign gods and their priestly representatives (I Kings 17-19). In both of these cases, early in the Old Testament, there is no common ground, and no appeal to some common principle (other than the commonality of agreeing on some form of battle to test superiority). These are wars which are meant to end in nothing less than unconditional surrender.[44]

But the Bible also narrates wisdom contests in which not only the power but also the wisdom of the gods is

---

44 Leeuwen, A. T. v. (1964). *Christianity in world history; the meeting of the faiths of East and West*. London, Edinburgh House Press. pp. 125-127. Van Leewen points out that with Pharoah there is no common ground. With the Caesar, Paul appeals to a certain kind of common ground. In all of our encounters, we were dealing with "half Christians," and therefore they immediately see a kind of "common ground."

challenged. With both Joseph and Daniel, we find God has providentially placed His own prophets in the court of the king (Genesis 40-41, Daniel 1-2, 4). In both cases, the Pharaoh, or the king, is confronted with a nightmare or enigma (as in the case of the handwriting on the wall in Daniel 5) that is incomprehensible. The wise men of the court are incapable of acting as interpreters, and it is at the most crucial point that the prophet of Jehovah is called upon, and he is capable of acting as an interpreter. In both instances, the wisdom of the true God triumphs, and once again the gods are vanquished. When the gods are vanquished, their representatives are also vanquished, and the heart of the king is either won or he is conquered. Pharaoh and Nebuchadnezzar were both vanquished and both became God-fearers.[45] The nightmares of leaders are our opportunity and believe me God is so good that He will send nightmares to all leaders. These nightmares are opportunities. The question then is how does one understand and interpret the nightmare?

In the New Testament, Paul takes up this theme in I Corinthians 1:18-25:

"[18] For the message of the cross is foolishness to those who are perishing, but to us who are being saved it is the power of God. [19] For it is written:

I will destroy the wisdom of the wise,

And bring to nothing the understanding of the prudent.

[20] Where is the wise? Where is the scribe? Where is the disputer of this age? Has not God made foolish the wisdom of this world? [21] For since, in the wisdom of God, the world through wisdom did not

---

45 Jordan, J. B. (2007). *The Handwriting on the Wall: A Commentary on the Book of Daniel.* Powder Springs. GA, American Vision. pp. 231-267

know God, it pleased God through the foolishness of the message preached to save those who believe. [22] For Jews request a sign, and Greeks seek after wisdom; [23] but we preach Christ crucified, to the Jews a stumbling block and to the Greeks foolishness, [24] but to those who are called, both Jews and Greeks, Christ the power of God and the wisdom of God. [25] Because the foolishness of God is wiser than men, and the weakness of God is stronger than men."

Power and wisdom contests reached their zenith in the death and resurrection of Jesus. God vanquished all of His enemies, transforming many, demonstrating both that He is more powerful than they, and that He is infinitely wiser. Our baptism is a baptism into both the death and resurrection of Christ (Romans 6:1-11, Colossians 2:12). If we are baptized into Him, then we partake of these victories, and extend them. We participate in His spoils. Hence, the Old Testament foreshadowings are fulfilled in Christ, and Old Testament figures who function as types, such as Moses, Elijah, Joseph and Daniel, give us guidance and direction for the further extension of the final victory that has now been won in the death and resurrection of Christ (Luke 24:13-27). This also indicates that victory can only come now to the Christian (whether a pastoral advisor or an official) through trial, suffering and even death. Initial attention getters invariably lead later to great difficulties that can only be overcome through faith and endurance in Jesus Christ.

Under what circumstances are power and wisdom contests carried out? In order to understand this, we need an overview of Old Testament history. Hang on to your hats for this whirlwind tour.

THREE CONFIGURATIONS OF HUMAN SOCIETY IN THE OLD TESTAMENT

There are three configurations of the human ordering of society in the Old Testament, and these three broadly outline for us all types of societies that exist.[46] From Judges through the time of Israel's appointment of Saul to be king, Israel is a tribal configuration. From the time of Saul and David through the time of Zedekiah, when Judah goes into captivity, Israel is a monarchy, and city and town life begin to come to a new importance. Then, from the time of the Babylonian Captivity to the end of the Old Testament, through the time of the coming of Christ, the world is dominated by great multi-cultural empires, and cities assume a very central prominence.[47]

Each one of these eras has a typical sin that overshadows others in seriousness. The tribal era is dominated by sins against the father on the part of the son, or sins of the father against the son. The typical sin of the monarchical era is brother/brother rivalry. The typical sin of the empire era is the sin of false intermarriage. We see this repeated several times through the Old Testament in spiraling ways.

We first see this in the book of Genesis when Adam sins against his Father, the rivalry of Cain against Abel and the intermarriage of the sons of God with the daughters of men before the Flood. This is then repeated and corrected with Abraham being obedient to his Father (the Lord God) for

---

46 Ibid.
   pp. 29-37

47 Jordan, J. B. (1994). *Crisis, Opportunity, and the Christian Future*. Niceville, FL, Transfiguration Press.

many years while waiting for a son to be conceived. We see sibling rivalry between both Isaac and Ishmael and Jacob and Esau, and yet there is no fratricide. And, finally, we see Joseph marry the daughter of the High Priest of Egypt, but there is no hint in the text of sin. One ought to conclude that Asenath became (like Pharaoh and much of Egypt) a true convert.

The pattern repeats with the tribal era of the Judges sinning against God as their Father through repeated idolatries, the brotherly rivalry of Saul with David and the false and destructive intermarriage of Solomon with his many wives particularly in the rivalry between the southern and the northern kingdoms in Judah and Israel and then, in the Empires of the Captivity era, the struggle with false intermarriage in both Ezra and Nehemiah.[48]

EMPIRES

An emperor is a king of kings. There is an historical development that leads to this end. Tribes are ruled by chiefs. Then something like national boundaries can begin to grow up when a king unites a number of tribes under his own rule. Thus a king is a chief of chiefs. Finally, large human configurations develop when an emperor unites a number of kingdoms under a single rule. Thus, an emperor is a king of kings.

Empires are multi-cultural and usually multi-linguistic configurations. In empires, the greater the diversity of culture and language, the less that is held in common

---

48 Jordan, J. B. (2007). *The Handwriting on the Wall: A Commentary on the Book of Daniel*. Powder Springs. GA, American Vision. p. 34

among all of the peoples. Empires become thin in terms of commonalities. It is impossible to hold so many cultural and linguistic diversities together apart from considerable tolerance. But, at a certain point, tolerance can increase to such an extent that it becomes paradoxical in effect.

Tolerance ceases to enable diverse peoples to cooperate and becomes a firewall that separates peoples from one another. Peoples cease to have enough in common to meaningfully function together in a body politic, and new danger arises as each group ceases to be citizens of an empire and begins to again function separately and finally as distinct tribes. Another term for this is Balkanization.

THE CRISIS OF ORIENTATION

Within an empire, there is a crisis of orientation. There is not enough agreed upon cultural content to give direction and common consent to the large bodies of diverse people who are forced to function together. The gods are indeed at war and no god reigns with any supremacy. Hence, no one knows what to do.

The power of empires is very great, but either the will or capacity to use power is lacking. Action requires certain orientation, and this is just what becomes scarce in these situations.

Intermarriage is symbolic of what plagues all empires.[49] Empires welcome competing worldviews and value systems into the chambers of government. As a result, empires

---

49 It must be emphasized, the intermarriage being spoken of is not racial or even national. It is religious, and points to someone inside the Covenant marrying someone outside of it, and ultimately one polytheist marrying another polytheist, which is chaos intermingling with chaos.

become very broad and orientation becomes a crisis. Nobody believes in anything with very much fervor, or if they do they become an unwelcome thorn in a bed of tolerance. Believing in all gods is the same as believing in none of them.

The one time in Israel's history when it approached an empire status was during its monarchical era under the reign of Solomon. Solomon's reign was marred by intermarriage to foreign women who worshipped many gods. Much later in both Ezra 9-10 and Nehemiah 13:23-31, false intermarriage is again the major issue with which Israel must struggle.

Intermarriage with foreign women, who are idol worshippers, while an issue in itself, points to the larger issue of pluralism and syncretism in all empires. Empires in their decadent and dying stages become helpless giants, incapable of acting, or even protecting themselves, in spite of massive available power and wealth. Like Solomon, they have a thousand wives all worshipping different gods at different altars, advising him what to do. One simply ceases to act and one becomes a passive, reactive giant.[50]

---

50 There is a stage even beyond intermarriage in empires, and that is the stage that glorifies the homoerotic. I have written a paper entitled *The Gospel of John, Friendship, and the Homoerotic* that examines this question. Friendship was almost exclusively a Greek ideal, and it is not until the outpouring of the Holy Spirit that friendship ceases to be "too hot to handle." The Holy Spirit now becomes the new bond between same sex friends instead of the erotic as it was for the Greek. Homosexuality becomes even more disorienting in late empires than polygamous marriage to idolatrous women. It is the final stage of decadence. I believe John's Gospel was written self consciously into this issue and as an answer to it. It is the Gospel of friendship. It brings cure to the Greek.

POWER AND WISDOM CONTESTS

As stated earlier, God demonstrates both His superior power and His superior wisdom in the context of challenging enemies and rivals of the Kingdom.[51] The Bible gives examples of both power and wisdom contests in all three configurations. In tribal and monarchical eras, the crisis is usually one of power, and as one might expect power contests dominate those times. Tribal war and civil war are the major problems of tribal and monarchical eras and are the result of inequality of power. However, in empire eras, power is readily at hand, but in empire eras the lack of orientation is the crisis, and as one might expect wisdom contests predominate.

Thus, in the time of Pharaoh in Joseph's life, and in the time of Nebuchadnezzar in Daniel's life (both set in empires, nightmares come to the king, and he does not know what to do. Joseph and Daniel give orientation to the king with wisdom that triumphs over the pluralistic advisors who surround the king. Jehovah thus becomes the God of the empire and proves Himself large enough to encompass it.[52]

It certainly is true that when murderous and rivalrous

---

51 The creation account of Genesis 1-2 can be seen as a power and wisdom demonstration against all near eastern rival accounts, which can only give narrations of finite and limited gods. The entire account of the Exodus is, outside of the death and resurrection of Christ, the power contest *par excellence.* The Prophets are frequently structured as wisdom contests. Isaiah challenges the gods and enemies of Jehovah to "set forth your case...", and declare what is to happen (Isaiah 41:21-24)

52 Jordan, J. B. (2007). *The Handwriting on the Wall: A Commentary on the Book of Daniel.* Powder Springs. GA, American Vision. pp. 190-192. The true God is both one and many (Tri-une) in His reality, and thus large enough, unified, and many or plural all at once. Only the true God is adequate for an empire.

factions arise to challenge the supremacy of Daniel, and of Shadrack, Meshach and Abed-Nego, then power contests prove the supremacy of the God of the Jews over the local gods of the rival factions. Both wisdom and power contests are in view, but primacy is given to power in tribal and monarchical eras, and primacy is given to wisdom in empire eras.

Power contests are secondary to wisdom contests in the greatest achievements in the empire setting. Most of these encounters, however, involve power contests at some point, and some of them do not move much beyond that level. The relationship develops beyond initial involvement, the crisis becomes orientation. The power encounter seems essentially to function as an attention getter. If that is moved beyond, the relationship begins to take on dimensions of being an advisor or a counselor.[53] Now to return to the question, "How does one become an advisor to the king?" How does someone in a very pluralistic and syncrestic situation begin to function in truth? To ask it another way, "What are the marks of the times, as the tribe of Issachar were able to discern in their own time?"

---

53 In our local context, the pastors on a number of occasions, prayed for impossible situations on the part of public officials, and we saw (often to our surprise) remarkable answers to prayer on their behalf. Most of these were essentially power contest situations (although the boundary between power and wisdom contests is a fuzzy boundary). These were attention getters and in some cases led to much deeper relationships which opened the way to the need for wisdom in the midst of conundrums. We prayed for such things as peace in certain inter-collegial sports rivalries that often led to fights and even riots for a law enforcement official, opened communication with Islamic student groups for a university official after 9/11, openness on the part of a hostile city council to the need for expansion for a homeless shelter. In all of these cases, the answers that came were swift and surprising to a stunning degree.

TRIBALISM, MONARCHY, EMPIRE: HOPE, LOVE, AND FAITH

The advisor to the king needs to identify the current environment and historical circumstance of the king. Where is the civic leader developed in the three fold configurations of in the Bible? The three eras of the Old Testament period (tribal, monarchical, empire) become the prototype for the church era, and civil history develops in similar fashion.[54]

The Apostle Paul says that there are three things that abide: faith, hope and love (I Corinthians 13:13). It is useful to see these three theological virtues as being lead virtues in the three eras of Church history. This does not mean that all three virtues are not at work at every period in history, but rather that each era has a lead virtue that tends to lead people into the Kingdom of God, because it is the most deeply felt need.

The historical order is, however, different from St. Paul's order. The historical order is hope, love and finally faith.

ROMAN EMPIRE AND HOPE

The late collapsing Roman Empire was a time of the collapse of hope. Cochrane's *Christianity and Classical Culture* demonstrates that an overwhelming sense of fate hung like a dead weight over the dying Classical world. Classicism and paganism had tried and done everything, and there was nowhere left to go. Hopelessness and a desperate

---

54 Jordan, J. B. (1994). *Crisis, Opportunity, and the Christian Future*. Niceville, FL, Transfiguration Press.

sense of futility and vicious circularity encompassed the dying world of Rome.[55]

EUROPEAN TRIBES AND LOVE

As the Roman world collapsed, the tribes moved in and attacked civilization almost as a parasite on a host body. The northern tribes were then slowly evangelized by the monks. The very characteristic of tribes is that each tribe considers itself as the only people. Those outside of the tribe are fit only to be raped, enslaved or killed. The monks taught the tribes the Law of God, and it came as good news to them.[56] Paul says that "he who loves has fulfilled the Law," (Romans 13:8). The Law taught them that instead of dozens of different gods, all in competition and at war with each other, there was only one God, and each tribe was to worship the same God. And as a result the love of God united hearts and, consequently, the tribes. The Law taught that it was no longer acceptable to steal other men or to steal other men's wives just because they belonged to a different tribe. It taught that one could no longer covet the possessions of other men, and even the goods of men of other tribes. And the best news of all was that Jesus' blood was the one sufficient sacrifice; the blood of enemies was no longer needed to slake blood thirst. The Law brought new order and taught men how to live in new and better ways. It taught men how to love and what the content of love was. St. Paul tells us that "...love is the fulfilling of the Law," (I Corinthians 13:10b).

---

55 Cochrane, C. N. (1957). *Christianity and classical culture.* New York, Oxford University Press. pp. 456-516

56 Jordan, J. B. (1994). *Crisis, Opportunity, and the Christian Future.* Niceville, FL, Transfiguration Press. p. 12-18

In effect, the tribes were taught the first two offices of the Law (the Law as the revelation of the good in interpersonal relationships, and the Law as a revelation of what civil law ought to be).

EUROPEAN MONARCHISM AND FAITH

After approximately 700 years, the Law ceased to be good news. The third office of Law (the law as condemnation) took real effect in the hearts of men. The Law ceased to be good news and became bad news. Luther found the Law as that which condemned and it was unbearable.[57] It was faith that gave Luther the way out of his dilemma of condemnation. His great discovery was justification by faith, and it gave him a way out of the power of guilt.

EMPIRES AND HOPE

But today, the Lutheran Gospel no longer speaks to the western world. People neither know that there is a God or that He is offended and that forgiveness is the great necessity. Rather, we resemble the sociology of the collapsing Roman Empire more than at any time in the last 1500 years.

We are living in a time of the collapse of hope. The novels and stories of Franz Kafka, for example, illustrate the sense of the dead weight of fate and hopelessness

---

57 Schaff, P. (1983). *The creeds of Christendom : with a history and critical notes.* Grand Rapids, MI, Baker Book House. p. 640

Gill, J. (1971). *A Body of Divinity.* Grand Rapids, Michigan, Sovereign Grace Publishers. p. 367-372

which many modern people feel.[58] Much of what is at the heart of this collapse of hope is a collapse of community and relationship. Isolation and loneliness seem to be the accompaniment to the collapse of hope.

Great decaying empires all seem to come to the impasse of intense hopelessness and sense of futility.[59] Even the will to live, or to even exist, comes to be undermined. In the great Eastern empires of India and China, the feeling of despair is countered by the great Eastern mysticisms of Hindu Brahmanism, Buddhism and Taoism. Herein the ideal is entry into a state of either non-differentiated oneness, or non-existence. Confucianism is also a philosophy of social numbness[60] The late Roman Empire likewise idealized a non-feeling state in the pantheism of the Stoics as exemplified in the life and Meditations of Marcus

---

58 Kafka, F., W. Muir, et al. (1992). *The castle*. New York, Knopf ; Distributed by Random House.

Kafka, F. and J. Neugroschel (1993). *The metamorphosis and other stories*. New York, Charles Scribner's Sons.

Kafka, F. (1957). *The trial*. New York,, Knopf.

Jordan, J. B. (1994). *Crisis, Opportunity, and the Christian Future*. Niceville, FL, Transfiguration Press. p. 35-36

59 I am struggling with how to best say this, because in actuality, hope is a biblical virtue, and does not in any full sense exist outside of an encounter with Jehovah. Many authors have made the point that "the future" was "invented" by the Hebrew prophets. Rosenstock-Huessy, E. (1947). The Christian future : or the modern mind outrun. London, S.C.M. Press. p. 63

Newbigin, L. (1989). *The Gospel in a pluralist society*. Grand Rapids, Mich. Geneva [SZ], W.B. Eerdmans ;

WCC Publications. p.101

But it is still the case that in all paganisms, there comes a point of a sense of futility that is overwhelming, and there is no point even in existence. Hence, the sense of circularity of paganism in other configurations and times is not one that destroys the "will to live" or a childlike joy that frequently is observable in tribal and pagan settings.

60 Rosenstock-Huessy, E. (1947). *The Christian future : or the modern mind outrun*. London, S.C.M. Press. pp. 42-53

Aurelius.[61] Decaying empires in combating hopelessness will either take refuge in the aristocratic numbness of Brahmin or Stoical indifference or will engage in orgies of feeling that are devoid of the severe discipline of the tribe and only momentarily cathartic.[62] Combinations of both possibilities are moved between. It is easy to see analogies to our modern situation. The great power of the Church at this point is the power that she has to restore hope and with it relationship and community.[63]

Hope is not something that is immediately amenable to will. There are two things that are amenable to will that will give rise to hope if they are intentionally pursued before the face of God. The first is grief in a time of loss, and the second is gratitude in all circumstances, whether that circumstance is one of happiness or sadness. Repressed grief in the face of loss will stymie the renewed growth of hope. And the conscious expression of gratitude in all circumstances will give rise to hope since the practice of thanksgiving is a practical expression of belief in God's

61 Cochrane, C. N. (1957). *Christianity and classical culture*. New York, Oxford University Press. pp. 165ff

Marcus, A., J. Moore, et al. (2008). *The meditations of the Emperor Marcus Aurelius Antoninus*. Indianapolis, Liberty Fund.

62 The sexual and mordant orgies of the Games and Amphitheatre of the dying Roman Empire are legendary. "Sex and death" became the preoccupations of large portions of the population at that time as huge, lavish, squanderings of wealth were poured out to pre-occupy what might otherwise be a revolutionary population. These games even went on while the tribes were ravaging the Empire, and not a finger was lifted. It seemed nothing was left that was worth fighting for. But the population were allowed to feel. See Mannix, D. P. (1958). *Those About to Die*. New York, Ballantine Books.

63 Jordan, J. B. (1994). *Crisis, Opportunity, and the Christian Future*. Niceville, FL, Transfiguration Press.

overarching sovereignty and a belief that in that sovereignty God is working all things for His glory and my good.[64]

In regard to grief, it is no mistake that The Book of Lamentations follows the destruction of Jerusalem and the loss of Israel. If Israel can grieve, then hope can be restored.[65] Thus, grief and gratitude give rise to hope, and hope gives rise to the rebirth of community. Community is in large measure shared hope.[66] To state it boldly, the rebirth of hope and community is not possible apart from the Church and the Christian faith. This reality is very much a cornerstone of the advisor to the king, and is a great source of his boldness in his position. Apart from the God of the Bible, there is no one to grieve before in any adequate way or anyone to be grateful to. Israel survived centuries of captivity with the Lamentations, Psalms, and the Prophets

---

64 Carothers, M. R. (1998). *Power in Praise*. Escondia, CA, M.R. Carothers.

65 "You, O Lord, remain forever;
   Your throne from generation to generation.
   Why do you forget us forever,
   And forsake us for so long a time?
   Turn us back to You, O Lord, and we will be restored;
   Renew our days as of old,
   Unless You have utterly rejected us,
   And are very angry with us!" (Lamentations 5:19-22 NKJV)

66 All of this points to the recurring importance of the Psalms, which are especially tribal in their outlook. The intense, but disciplined feeling that is expressed all through the Psalms, has always maintained a centrality through both all of Israel's history, and through all of Church history, no matter what configuration of society one is currently within. Nothing could be more important than the revival of the Psalms in a late empire era. Intense feeling of grief, anger, joy, and thankfulness must be refound and re-expressed. Nothing points to the decadence of our churches more than the decline of the use of the Psalms and the rise of the syrupy, sentimental, and the eroticised in our worship. Those who have conquered and reconquered a hostile world, from the Benedictines to the Scottish Covenanters, have always been Psalm singers.

as their guides to grief, gratitude, hope and consequent community.

GLOBAL EMPIRE AND TRIBALISM AS ANODYNES TO ONE ANOTHER

The suggestion has been made that in the Christian era we are in a period when every form of government co-exists at the same time,[67] but now we are entering a time when we see particularly the co-existence of empire and tribe. A great world wide global economic empire is developing before our eyes, and at the same time we see the rousing of tribalism in the African, Asian and Middle Eastern world, and neo-tribalism is growing everywhere in the developed world.[68] These are acting as anodynes to one another. The global economic empire links the entire world together in markets and in corporations that are transnational, and yet this engine of cheap consumer goods and transnational manufacturing and services is also very impersonal and faceless. In reaction to this are intense and small tribal groupings that are personal and marked by immediate and fervent relationship. There is a great reductionistic drive to characterize our world as either

---

67 Rosenstock-Huessy, E. (1938, reprinted 1969). *Out of Revolution; Autobiography of Western Man*. Norwich, VT., Argo Books. pp. 453-455

68 "Neo-tribalism" would include the rebirth of small clubs and groups that are bound together by common interests and friendship, as well as renewed interest in blood relationships and the extended family. This is behind the drive to discover "roots." Various cults are particularly focused on family and blood relationships, like Mormonism, and even Islam. Gangs in our inner cities are essentially tribal. It almost goes without saying that the Church is the true form of the tribe. It developed with a tribal structure and this is why some church governments have centrally elders as rulers.

a growing empire configuration, or tribal configuration. Following Eugen Rosenstock-Huessy,[69] it is both at once, and only by reckoning on both, can one account for world-wide developments and needs.[70] This has been a vital idea that I have related to every leader I have ever interacted with. All leaders have to orient themselves to a world that encompasses not only Europe and North America, but also Africa, India, China and the Middle East, with massive immigrant populations, many of them tribal in origin and orientation, teeming into the Western world. The simple idea that we are seeing both the tribal and the empire at once as anodynes gives an almost instant orientation to what is otherwise a completely confusing polyglot of populations. City and university officials all over America are dealing with both all of the time, but have never been able to see any coherence in those patterns. With this the puzzle begins to come into focus.

THE SUBORDINATION OF THE STATE, AND THE UNIVERSITY TO THE CITY

The two major institutions which have developed over the last one thousand years are the nation state and the university. In both of these institutions the diseases of modernity are rampant. The dilemma of the repression of the Kingdom of God and of the privatization of the

---

69   Rosenstock-Huessy is the author who has had more influence on the writer of this project than probably any other. See Appendix I for a biographical account of him.

Eugen Rosenstock-Huessy (1888-1973). Volume, DOI: http://www.argobooks. org/biography.html

70   This point will be extensively developed in the fifth chapter

Christian religion are notable in both. Attempts to cope with and transform the pluralism of our times into a foundational fact is a bottom-line enterprise.

Now, however, both the university and the nation state are becoming subordinate to the development of the city. It is in the city that the schizophrenia and the repressed reality of the Kingdom of God, have the greatest potential to be resolved. It is in the city that the Church will once again reconfigure its authority and become the servant-authority. It is at this level that advisor to the king can have the greatest effect and reintegrate the kingdom of God into the structures and institutions of the world.

HOW WE ARE APPROACHING THE END AND A NEW BEGINNING

The familiar benediction found at the end of the third chapter of Paul's Epistle to the Ephesians reads:

> [20] Now to Him who is able to do exceedingly abundantly above all that we ask or think, according to the power that works in us, [21] to Him be glory in the church by Christ Jesus to all generations, forever and ever. Amen.

A literal translation of the phrase "to all generations" would be "in the age of ages." The age of Jesus Christ is the age of ages. What this phrase implies is that the era of the New Covenant is dominated by the risen and ascended Christ. This is His age and within this age there are distinct ages, and, even if our reading of these eras is not perfect, we can be assured that a search for historical order is not futile.

Distinct eras can be discerned in the Old Covenant.[71] The figures of Adam, Noah, Abraham, Moses and David are major figures through whom God created and renewed the covenant with His people. Minor figures, through which each of these covenants is renewed, can also be clearly seen. In the era of the Judges, for example, which was initiated by Moses' successor, Joshua, we see the covenant renewed by figures like Deborah, Gideon, Jephthah and Sampson.

It is also the case that covenant renewal is not predicated on human initiative, or even ultimately on obedience. Jehovah over and over again demonstrates His sovereignty and goodness in renewing the covenant with His people after periods of prolonged disobedience. The transition from the era of the Judges to the era of the Monarchy was not initiated by God because of the deserving obedience of Israel. In fact, it is just the opposite. Israel's initial demand for a king was prompted out of a desire to be like the nations and the text explicitly states that it was a result of rejecting Jehovah as King over them (I Samuel 8:5,7). As a result, for forty years Israel must endure Saul as a bad monarch, after which God not only renews His covenant with Israel, but the covenant that He establishes is far more glorious and wonderful than His previous covenant with Israel through Judges.

As James Jordan says:

"We have stated that there is always a decline that partially explains the need for a new covenant. It is also true,

---

71 Jordan, J. B. (1988). *Through new eyes : developing a Biblical view of the world.* Brentwood, Tenn., Wolgemuth & Hyatt. p.165-289
Robertson, O. P. (1980). *The Christ of the covenants.* Grand Rapids, Baker Book House.

however, that even if man had not sinned there would have been advances from glory to glory. Thus, the coming of a new covenant is not wholly to be explained by the failure of the previous one. Also involved is the fact of human maturation, so that what was once appropriate and fitting at a certain stage of childhood now must be superseded. As children grow, we have to keep getting them new shoes and new clothing, partially because the old ones are wearing out, but also because the child has outgrown them.

This explains why God never simply calls His people back to the previous covenant... Rather, it is a renewal of the old ways in a new form, a form appropriate to the times and to the stage of growth."[72]

Just as recognizable covenant renewals came through the entire Old Testament period, Jesus Christ has now inaugurated the New Covenant, and a similar pattern should be expected throughout the New Covenant era. Indeed, this is precisely what the age of ages is.

The question now arises, how in the Christian economy have we arrived at the primacy of the city, and does that arrival function to give the hope and renewal and new life to the king? Are we at the threshhold of a Covenant Renewal in God's plan for the world, and can the king take hope in this?

THE INITIAL GOODNESS OF THE CITY

Empires are a conglomeration of a series of cities or even city states. This new ideal we are speaking of is the city, but not just any city, and not the city of Athens, or the city

---

72 Jordan, J. B. (1988). *Through new eyes : developing a Biblical view of the world.* Brentwood, Tenn., Wolgemuth & Hyatt. p.181

of Rome. Rather, it is the City of God, the New Jerusalem.

We see this already dawning on humanity. We hear everywhere about the global city. But we must give content to this city that is vaguely envisioned. The 21st and 22nd chapters of Revelation give us this outline, and this is the outline that must be given to our world.

Here are two contrasting visions of the city. The French sociologist and theologian,[73] Jacques Ellul wrote a book length theology of the city, *The Meaning of the City*.[74] Ellul for a number of years wrote books in tandem, He would first write a book from a sociological perspective, and, following that, he would write a book on the same theme from a theological perspective. In 1964, Ellul's *The Technological Society* was translated and published in English.[75] A few years later, he published *The Meaning of the City* as a theological corollary. Ellul is famously pessimistic, especially in regard to technology. Ellul mocks the idea that technology is only as good or bad as its users. He views technology as exercising a logic of its own that is determinative over human choice. Hence, human choice

---

73 Ellul was a professional sociologist and an "amateur" theologian. But "amateur" hardly has a demeaning sense here. Amateur, in its original meaning, means that one does something for the love of the activity, and not for money. Some "amateurs" give every cause to "professionals" to quail in their boots on the question of competence. C.S. Lewis refused to take money for any lecture he did on theology, because he was not a professional. He only too gladly took money to lecture on medieval literature and the medieval world, because, there he was a professional. But Lewis, like Ellul, would be very likely to vanquish any professional opponent on the field of theological battle.

74 . Ellul, J. (1970). *The meaning of the city*. Grand Rapids,, Eerdmans.

75 . Ellul, J. (1964). *The technological society*. New York, Vintage Books.

is not sovereign over technology. Rather, technology determines human choice. His later study of the city in the light of his reading of the biblical revelation confirms his pessimism in this regard.

Ellul's book begins with the ominous sentence, "The first builder of the city was Cain."[76] This in effect tells the whole story, and the rest of the book is an elucidation of this first and dark sentence. Ellul continues with his city narrative, that after Cain murders his brother, he is marked by God, and he escapes "away from the presence of the Lord to the land of Nod, east of Eden" ("the land of wandering, or nowhere"). And again, "Once settled in his country, Cain does two things to make his curse bearable: he knows his wife sexually, who then gives him a son; and he builds a city."[77] The first city, according to Ellul, was the city of Enoch, first built by Cain after he murdered his brother, Abel. His descendants, Jubal and Tubal-Cain were the pioneers of the arts (Jubal was the father of those who play the flute and the harp) and metallurgy (Tubal-Cain, was the first craftsman in iron and bronze). Thus, Ellul sees cities, culture and technology, through this pessimistic lens. All of these have their origins in the line of the seed of the serpent.

Ellul does see the obvious fact that redemption ends in a city. But he only grants the final goodness of this as a concession on the part of God toward the human race. The city has its origins in human anxiety and the response of man to that anxiety is to seek security apart from God in a collective existence. Hence, according to Ellul, the city has

---

76   . Ellul, J. (1970). *The meaning of the city*. Grand Rapids,, Eerdmans. p. 1

77   . Ibid. p.5

its origin in sin.[78]

I would challenge this characterization. Ellul would be correct if Enoch were indeed the first city. Then the characterization that the world begins in a Garden paradise that is essentially rural but ends in a city in the New Jerusalem would also be correct. Rather, I contend that the first city or, more accurately the first protocity, is Eden itself.

The urbanologist, Jane Jacobs, in her volume The Economy of Cities, challenges a number of the prevailing perspectives on the city.[79] She challenges the idea that the first economies were rural and that only gradually does the country give way to the village and then to the town and the city and this can only happen after a surplus of agricultural goods is produced. Rather, she contends that everything we know about how economies develop indicate they first developed in the city and were then transferred to the country. She points out that the most advanced agricultural economies in the world are found in the most citified

---

78 . "Such is the meaning of the Bible as a book written by men. God did not adopt an original means to reveal himself. No, he expressed his revelation in the forms and modes invented by man for his own affairs. And this is also the meaning of God's decision *to take over for himself man's invention of the city.* (Emphasis added) God does not reject the world of revolt and death, he does not annhilate it in the abyss of fire. Rather, he adopts it. That is, he takes charge of it. And the immense vanity that man put into it, God transforms into a city with gates of pearl. Thus, and only thus, does our work take on meaning, both significance and direction. No longer is it a vanity among vanities. No longer is it a permanent return to nothingness. Civilizations pass and go under, leaving a few ruins buried by vines, and the stones lose their grip and fall in silence. But nothing is forgotten. All the pain and hope represented by these walls is taken over by God. And because of it all, God is preparing this same setting for man, but made new. And because of all this in God's plan, his Jerusalem will be the fulfillment of all that man expected." p. 176

79 . Jacobs, J. (1969). *The economy of cities.* New York,, Random House.

nations, and the most backward agricultural economies are found in those areas and nations that have the fewest and least developed economies. Farm economies grow first in cities and are transferred to the rural areas. All evidence increasingly indicates that cities are very early. They are not late in the development of any society, but come very close to the outset of cultures.[80]

Hence, I would suggest that the original city was not Enoch, but the original city was Eden. Eden was the original sanctuary. The center of every city is its temple. The city is the religious center of the surrounding areas. Hence, the first city is not Enoch, but Eden.

The heart of the city is religious before it is economic.[81]

---

80 Ibid. "One of many surprises I found in the course of this work was especially unsettling because it ran counter to so much I had always taken for granted. Superficially, it seemed to run counter to common sense and yet there it was: work that we usually consider rural has originated not in the countryside, but in cities. Current theory in many fields—economics, history, anthropology—assumes that cities are built upon a rural economic base. If my observations and reasoning are correct, the reverse is true: that is, rural economies, including agricultural work, are directly built upon city economies and city work.

"So thoroughly does the theory (in my view, the dogma) of agricultural primacy saturate the conventional assumptions about cities that I propose to deal with it in this chapter as the first order of business.

"We are all well aware from the history of science that ideas universally believed are not necessarily true. We are also aware that it is only after the untruth of such ideas has been exposed that it becomes apparent how pervasive and insidious their influence has been." pp. 3-4

81 The economies of both the final two cities at the end of the book of Revelation as Babylon the Great, and The New Jerusalem are indistinguishable from their worship. Gold, silver, precious stones and human beings either represent idolatrous and vile adulterous worship, or are entirely dedicated to the worship of the true God in even the lowest of human activities. We see, for example, the great harlot drinking from a golden sacramental cup a drink of abominations and filthiness in Babylon the Great, or the pavement which is walked upon is made of pure gold in the New Jerusalem. (Revelation 17-18 and 21-22)

The final city, the New Jerusalem, is without a temple or cathedral at its center because the whole of the city is a temple. It is a perfect cube, which was the shape the Holy of Holies in the Tabernacle and Temple. In the New Jerusalem, there is no split or separation in worship and all other human activities. All have perfectly merged in communion and worship of God. All of human action is then done perfectly to the glory of God, and all of human action is a perfect sacrifice. This begins in every city with some form of worship and some form of temple being the city center. In the City of Man, the city is dedicated to humanity itself in self exaltation and worship.[82]

In Eden, the two trees are sacramental trees, and, hence, the two trees are in the center of the Garden and the most holy place. It is surrounded by the land of Eden, and outside of Eden is the world. This is a three layered universe (Sanctuary, Land, World) and it is reproduced extensively in the whole of the old economy of the Old Testament. It is reproduced later in both the Tabernacle and the Temple.[83] And the city of Jerusalem becomes Holy City Jerusalem.[84] If there had not been a fall, it seems likely that the world would first have developed in a population center around the sacramental trees of Eden. Scattering is originally a

---

82 It is possible for there to be sanctuaries that are in non-city settings (mountain tops, tree groves in rural settings, for example), but I am skeptical that it is possible for there to be cities without worship at their center. All of human action requires a bond, and it is the religious center that is that bond.

83 Jordan, J. B. (1988). *Through new eyes : developing a Biblical view of the world*. Brentwood, Tenn., Wolgemuth & Hyatt. pp. 143-163

84 Leithart, P. J. (2003). *From silence to song : the Davidic liturgical revolution*. Moscow, ID, Canon Press. Nehemiah 11:1, 18

curse imposed by God to weaken the collective power of idolatry human kind (Genesis 11:1-9).

If Eden is the first city (or protocity), then Ellul's characterization is robbed of its theological impetus, and Ellul's very negative characterization of the urban has its foundations taken from under it. The city is not a concession, but was the original plan of God that is restored in the New Jerusalem. The essence of the city is not evil and sin based at heart on anxious clustering together in hiddenness from God. Rather, the Tower of Babel element of the city is a perversion of an originally good structure.

Chapter Four

HOW THE COUNSELOR DEALS WITH THE NEUROSIS OF THE KING

I was sitting across the restaurant table from a law enforcement official in my city. A particularly sinister and twisted crime had been committed a number of months before and major scandal had ensued. "What do you think the chances are of this crime being solved?" I asked. "A very high percentage of all crimes of this type are solved. This one will be too," he said, but he said it with the cadence of Joe Friday, almost like an automaton. He was not persuasive. I could see the exhaustion and depression. It was visible.

This official and I had seen each other a number of times over the months. He seemed to enjoy my company and our conversation, but I felt he regarded me as some kind of religious, social worker. He more or less wanted my insights and loved my ideals but could not quite connect to my faith. In many ways he was the very embodiment of all that I have written about before. All of his ideals had ultimately come from the church he had left as an adolescent. He was filled with repressed Christian ideals. His idealism combined with his considerable competence made him ideal for his office in my city. But now he was up against intractable evil, and there seemed no resolution. I leaned forward, and I said, "Its time you let the pastors pray for you in some sort of systematic way about this." He leaned forward, and with what seemed almost infinite weariness said, "I don't want the pastors to pray for me. I want to pray for myself." With that, he soon dismissed himself and drove back to his office.

Later that day, I received a phone call. It was from him. On the ride back to his office, he had prayed. He prayed what I suppose we might call "a sinner's prayer." Whatever the exact contents of that prayer, God came, Christ came. He experienced the most remarkable and sudden conversion I have ever witnessed. He went from Saul to Paul in an instant.

Over the next weeks, I heard from him often. He saw God and God's hand everywhere. The Bible came alive. Life had an entirely new outlook. He went back to the church of his childhood.

The crime was never solved, and my friend passed through traumatic crisis in connection to it. He endured unbelievable stress over the next years, but had the strength to endure because of his faith. But in the end, my friend brought sustenance and renewal to his own department, and the renewal he brought to our city both in that office and in the years following can hardly be adequately chronicled. He became a Christian and became completed and at one with what before were schizophrenic ideals. He came to be at one with himself in a pluralistic world. He experienced a resurrection.[85]

---

85 My friend, through what had to have been supernatural endurance,

I have previously set forth the dilemmas and hidden tensions of this pluralistic world. These tensions are unconscious and form the fertile ground that makes possible, or even necessary, a pastoral approach to these people. But, as any pastoral counselor knows, one does not just announce to the counselee what his problem is. This would be futile and unhelpful. The counselee must come to see his or her own problems for themselves with the guidance of the counselor.

In the second section, I set forth the source of the ever present, but unrealized confusion, that is in the background. That confusion must be slowly unpacked and a solution must slowly be given. Much of what is referred to in chapter two may not be spoken of directly. It is akin to a psychiatric diagnosis. The diagnosis may guide the doctor, but direct discussion of the present illness is unhelpful, and discussion of diagnosis infamously gives rise to futile and endless intellectualizing that is counterproductive and never leads to change.[86] We cannot return to a prior Christendom, and the very idea of any attempt to do so will immediately be rejected by most modern leaders as impossible and absurd.

Modern pluralism may be problematic, but the modern leader sees it is a given. One must move forward from there and find solutions that do not suggest a simple move back to a past that is gone. Even if some form of renewed Christendom is the answer, it is usually futile to directly suggest that this is so. Even in Scripture, God sometimes acts by means of indirection or paradox that

survived in his office a full seven years before he resigned.

86 Glasser, W. (1975). *Reality Therapy, a new approach to psychiatry.* New York, Perennial Library. pp. 51-74

creates ways forward when no way forward seems possible and opens doors when no doors appear to even exist. The classic example is the Prophet Nathan's approach with the adulterous Kind David. Nathan first engages David in a seemingly unrelated issue, allows David to pass judgment, and then, and only then, does Nathan utter his famous line, "Thou art the man" (II Samuel 12:1-15). Paradox in Covenant Renewal in the Bible culminates in the Crucifixion and Resurrection which nobody understood at the time as God's ultimate way of bringing renewal.[87] Hence, much direct or extended discussion of the past destruction of Christendom and the rise of modernity is generally futile. In fact to the modern mind, the past Christendom and any hint of theocracy are more often than not the problem and disease to be overcome.[88] What is below are the assumptions behind what, over a period of time, is spoken. What is in this and the next chapter is much of the stuff of Wisdom Contests" when the wise men of the King's Court do not know what to say. How much of this is spoken, and how quickly, will depend on the depth of involvement, openness and opportunity between the pastoral counselor and the secular leader.

Just as Nathan had to approach the king by means of indirection and with wisdom, so today it is necessary for the advisor to approach the king with indirection and wisdom. Here are four motifs that enable the advisor to the king to approach the king with wisdom. The first is understanding

---

87   . I Corinthians 1:18-31, Hebrews 11

88   It should be noted that the world is already a theocracy, or perhaps more accurately, a Christocracy. When Christ ascended to the Right Hand of the Father, He inherited the nations, It is now a matter of whether we recognize this reality, or not.

and applying the death and resurrection motif of the Bible to the king. The second is understanding that the city is per se, not evil, but good and a part of God's creation ideal. The third is understanding that now the nation state and the university are going to be increasingly subordinate to the city. The fourth is understanding certain time cycles in history that are under God's control and understanding how God's actions in Covenant Renewals give us confidence and authority to press forward.

DEATH AND RESURRECTION MOTIF IN THE BIBLE

The entire backbone of this manifesto is the application of the biblical motif of death and resurrection to the leader's situation. This begins with his/her survival in office, but must then have a broader application than that. Eugen Rosenstock-Huessy has understood the death and resurrection motif as the key to Western history as no one has. For the life of the Church and the Kingdom of God when things appeared to be at dead ends, over and over, it turns out to be the beginnings.

We see this pattern in the Old Testament. God brought a wicked world to an end in the flood and saved only eight people in the ark. But the end of that first world carried the promise of the rainbow with it as God promised He would never again flood the earth and made a covenant with all living things (Genesis 9:8-17).

A few generations later, He initiates a program of redemption when He calls Abraham to Himself, and promises to bless the whole earth and all peoples in Him

(Genesis 12:1-3). This calling of Abraham is a calling that is over against universal judgment as He had exercised in the flood.

The family of Abraham develops for four generations, and then seventy people are called down into Egypt where eventually they are enslaved (Genesis 46:27). It is significant that seventy Hebrews go down into Egypt. Seventy is the number of the nations, being derived from the table of nations in Genesis 10. Whenever the number seventy arises, it is symbolic of the nations.[89] Egypt is a fiery furnace and slavery in Egypt is a kind of death. These Hebrew people are going down into Egypt to die for the world. Their enslavement is in place of a universal judgment that would once again destroy the earth. The Exodus is a resurrection. Israel emerges from the furnace of Egypt in new life and is raised from the dead by Yahweh. Israel now proceeds to explicitly become the priestly people to the entire world.

If the death/resurrection motif is not clear in the Egyptian experience, it is made explicit in the Babylonian captivity. Return from Babylon is directly likened to a resurrection in Ezekiel 37. This passage presents a vision of a valley of dry bones coming together, flesh coming onto the bones and breath entering the resurrected bodies. This is Israel and Israel is coming back from the dead.

Jesus literally fulfills the death and resurrection anticipated in Ezekiel 37, and the Church is baptized into His death and resurrection. The disciples are sent forth

---

89 An example of this would be in the Gospel of Luke, which is the Gospel to the Gentiles. In Luke 9, Jesus sends out the twelve to the Jews, which number is symbolic of Israel being the nation of twelve tribes. Then in Luke 10, He sends out seventy to cities He is preparing to go to, some of which are in Gentile areas, and include Gentiles.

to baptize in the name of the Father, the Son and the Holy Ghost, and they are to disciple the nations, not just individuals. Whole nations begin to take upon themselves this identity of "death and resurrection peoples" in analogous ways to Israel.

In previous chapters, we have spoken of the pattern of death and resurrection entering the life of the counselor to the king, as well as to the king himself. The hope for the leader is that his own experience of death and resurrection can become the experience of the institution he has headship over. Each institution is partaking of an era of a particular form of death and resurrection. It is in this that Rosenstock-Huessy has seen so deeply into. Hence, it is the explication of these patterns that become a way of giving orientation and hope to leaders.

SCAPEGOATING AND CYCLICAL TIME: HOPELESSNESS AND HOPE

The first time I met privately with one of the leaders in our city, I said, "I am praying for you to make it in your office to seven years." I hardly had to say another word. This person was almost as far down the road on this issue as was I. She said, "Before I came here (she named an important official in another state) X said to me, 'When you get there, I want you to break the four year curse.' " Indeed, nobody had made it in this particular office for more than five years in nearly forty years. This was a very moving issue for the official. Momentarily, she appeared to be near tears. She was very touched. I then told her that her first year would be a honeymoon, the second a bit tougher and the sheen would be gone, and between the third and forth year, all hell would break loose. "If there isn't a crisis, one will be invented. They will attempt to crucify you." Several years later, a crisis indeed was invented. I got a call one evening, and it was the chief of staff wanting to know if I would see this person. A time was arranged, and I had a meal with her and her husband. We discussed the crisis. "How long have you been here?" She thought for a few moments. "Almost exactly three and a half years." (This is significant, because Christ was crucified at 42 months, or 3 1/2 years into His ministry).

A number of years later, I had meeting with another person in that same office. I began by saying, "You know, you have about one more year before they come after you." He got silent. He was a very seasoned politician in his previous life. He knew exactly what I meant. He then said three things. "You have been around here a long time, haven't you." It was a statement, not a question. I said, "Yes." "You've seen this before, haven't you." Again, it was a statement. "Yes." Then he did ask a question. "What sect are you from?" I told him my affiliation (Presbyterian). He was very silent and thoughtful, and our interview ended. I never saw him again, but he resigned a few months later. When he left, he left with a hero's departure with the press trumpeting all that he had achieved. He had been there a little more than two years. What I knew was that he was getting out of Dodge ahead of the lynch mob that he knew was coming.

What follows in this section is not presented as a law, but as something that has typically functioned as one of the first acts of wisdom or interpretation that begins to win the king. The typical first act of wisdom in my experience has to do with a kind of prophesy regarding scapegoating and cyclical time.

This is the information that understandably has had the most immediate and often the deepest effect on almost all officials with whom I have counselled. This understanding is a combination of things that I have learned from Edwin Friedman, Rene Girard and James Jordan.[90]

Time is of the utmost in importance to anyone who is appointed or elected to any given office. As often as not, the reason someone is newly appointed or elected is to bring change and resolve problems that the institution has been experiencing. This, however, is not really the case. Institutions say they want change, but this is at best a schizophrenic desire. Change requires pain and nobody wants pain. Ray Bakke has said that the first rule of all pastoral care is that all change is experienced as loss, even if it means a net gain in the long run. People want change until it means change, and then what we all want is for the same tune to be played, with the hope that this time it will be different.

The Bible is replete with numbers and many numbers have a typological content. One of the most basic numbers is the number seven. The world was created in seven days,

90 Friedman, E. (1985). *Generation to generation : family process in church and synagogue*. New York, Guilford Press.

Bailie, G. (1995). *Violence unveiled : humanity at the crossroads*. New York, Crossroad.

Girard, R. (2001). *I see Satan fall like lightning*. Maryknoll, N.Y. Ottawa Leominster, Herefordshire, Orbis Books; Novalis; Gracewing.

Jordan, J. B. (2007). *The Handwriting on the Wall: A Commentary on the Book of Daniel*. Powder Springs. GA, American Vision.

and all through the Bible we find time being structured on sevens. Israel's long term calendar was so structured with a weekly Sabbath every seven days, a Sabbath year every seventh year and a Jubilee year every seven times seven years. The Gospel of John is extensively structured on sevens, as is the Book of Revelation, and Daniel prophesies about seventy weeks of years (7 X 10, Dan. 9:24).[91]

The number three and a half is obviously seven cut in two. We first find it employed when Elijah prays for it not to rain, and it does not rain for forty-two months, or three and a half years. Three and a half is a curse. It is a time of completion, of creation or recreation cut short or in two. (James 5:17, I Kings 18:1, Daniel 9:27, Revelation 11:2, 12:6, 13:5). Jesus was crucified at about three and a half years into His ministry. The implication is that His life was cut off or cut in two. He bore the curse for us.

When someone enters office, it will take somewhere between seven and ten years to bring meaningful renewal.[92] In our current environment, this almost never happens. Most leaders are cut off in the middle. In my experience, most leaders are effectively cut off before they have been in office for four years, and most will quit somewhere around five years. This means that renewal never takes place and that the old dysfunctions just continue. Most of our institutions are not being renewed, and at some point the

---

91 There are seven miracles and seven discourses in the Gospel of John, and Revelation has seven seals, seven trumpets, and seven bowls.

92 Rosenstock-Huessy, E. (1947). *The Christian future : or the modern mind outrun*. London, S.C.M. Press.
pp. -198-243 Cheyeny, T. *Climbing Past 400 In New Church Attendance*. Volume,   DOI: http://www.planterdude.com/media/CLIMBING_PAST_400_IN_NEW_CHURCH_ATTENDANCE.pdf

dysfunction could become complete.

In order to keep renewal from being brought by the leader, the leader must be removed or have his or her effectiveness destroyed. This happens through the process of blame and scapegoating. If a crisis can be found at hand, that will do. If one cannot be immediately found, one can always be manufactured. And this will happen with the greatest intensity somewhere between three and four years, at approximately three and a half years. In other words, the leader will be crucified. If he or she can survive this time, then they can make it to seven years, and be successful in bringing renewal. In this, they virtually pass through a resurrection.

If a resurrection is not experienced, then a new leader will be brought in, usually with great fanfare, to solve the problems that the previous leader could not resolve. What has really happened is that things are just going in vicious cycles, and the same thing in all likelihood will happen to the new leader. No real renewal will happen, and further decay and degeneration will continue to plague the institution, and will probably get worse.

CAPTURING THE CONSCIENCE OF THE KING

This forms the background of the capturing of the conscience of the king. Since the infamous 60s, when the fervor of the French Revolution was introduced into our universities and our cities, crucifixion of some sort is now almost inevitable in all positions of leadership in the United States.[93] In my experience, almost no leader in any

---

93 This is true in most parts of the country, except the Deep South and those

significant position lasts more than five years in his or her tenure. As an example, I have discovered as a result of my ministry that university presidents in this country routinely play a game of musical chairs about every four years. A deep intuitive knowledge exists, that it is impossible to survive in any presidential, or chancellor position, beyond an early era before conflict has developed. Leaving at four years is often a way of avoiding what appears to be inevitable destruction in that position. It is leaving ahead of the final and inevitable destruction and end of intolerable and impossible conflict that has by that time already been inaugurated.

My entry into many offices has been an understanding of this and speaking of this reality to the various leaders I have met. Understandably, there is hope of something better or more coming of what appears to be inevitable destructive conflict. Interest in talking with me is usually prompted by sheer self interest. People pursue these positions often for noble professional reasons, as well as sometimes, out of sheer personal ambition. Someone coming to them and speaking of an inevitable destruction of their position in office is certainly an attention getter. However, that discussion sometimes follows some kind of power encounter that has also been an attention getter. The prediction of the nightmare of coming conflict that will be utterly destructive is sometimes the first opening that the counselor has to begin to speak wisdom. Almost nobody else will broach such a subject, and, if they do, it is never broached with hope. Hope in the coming darkness is the

parts termed the Bible belt, which are still more stable. But in those parts of the country, the problem is often the opposite where officials stay and stay and form a good ol' boys' network that is just as impervious to renewal.

advisor to the king's great weapon and entrance. Who but a Christian, and particularly a Christian pastor, could better offer the hope of resurrection from the dead?

Chapter Five

THE FUTURE IS FOUND BY RECEDING INTO THE PAST WITH BIBLE IN HAND

We will now continue our schooling. Hold on, because this will not be easy sledding, but will continue to prepare you for what is out there and of how to speak wisdom after perhaps a power contest has gotten an official's attention. What has to be learned is how to interpret the nightmares that all officials are going to come up against. How can God's servant have something to say to the mysteries about which the court's wise men have nothing helpful to say? We will begin our journey through the great revolutions of the Western world, all in one way or another inspired by the Bible and the Christian faith, and form the background for who we are in the modern and now postmodern world. This will continue and deepen the biblical analysis that has preceded in this Manifesto. What is being unveiled in these revolutions are the real social layers that any leader in the city is actually dealing with in all of the institutions of modern society. The mysteries and the riddles of the social complexes of his or her time and place have their origins in these revolutions. An advisor to the king needs to have a credible rubric for orienting the king in the empire. The pluralism of all empires creates confusion and the greatest need is for orientation. Rosenstock-Huessy has in practice provided this for me. If one is to function as an advisor, the capacity to give orientation is absolutely essential. It may be that others who are called to this ministry may find other thinkers to be their guide, but Rosenstock-Huessy has for me been without peer in giving direction. To be consciously acquainted with the shape of these revolutions has provided indispensable direction as well as establishing the ethos of a credible rubric for understanding where history is going.

It is not arbitrary that we have arrived at this place of the centrality of the city. Eugen Rosenstock-Huessy outlines the tenets of this revolutionary development within Western history.[94] His theory moves beyond his own time and development (in the writer's opinion) into the city in the New Jerusalem.[95] This connects the development of Western history with the narrative of the Bible.

His mode of doing history was to examine the calendars, sermons, pamphlets and other documents of the contemporaries of those he was studying and to attempt to discover what their own understanding of who they were and where they were in time. He was distinctly interested in autobiography. Part of his excavation of time periods

[94] Rosenstock-Huessy, E. (1938, reprinted 1969). *Out of Revolution; Autobiography of Western Man*. Norwich, VT., Argo Books.

[95] Rosenstock-Huessy's great book, *Out of Revolution*, which was completed in 1939, ends with the Russian Revolution which is grounded in Genesis 1:1. In the writers opinion, having now completed one full sweep through the text of the Bible, we are now starting over again with the one pericope that is beyond the Last Judgment, and that is the great picture of the city in the New Jerusalem.

was to attempt to understand where contemporaries in any given era identified themselves in the text of the narrative of Scripture. Hence, we begin in the early medieval period with the Last Judgment and find that the Soviets and the free democracies of the 20th Century identified with the "Tohu and Bohu" of Genesis 1:3, Formless and Void. This constituted an entire move backward through the narrative of the Bible.

Here is a quotation from Rosenstock-Huessy from his great book, *Out of Revolution*:

"An efficient philology cannot believe in the material impenetrability of languages. It is not by chance that mankind restored its unity after the Babylonian confusion of tongues, by translating a single book into almost every tongue. The translation of the Bible into three hundred languages made up for man's loss of unity in speech. Furthermore, this restoration by common terms of thought was the cry and rallying point of every total revolution in Europe and America. So definitely is the revolutionary process of the last thousand years bound up with the unification of thought by the common possession of the Bible that every revolution passionately claimed a special section of Biblical history as the classical text for its own drama."

"The Popes of the Gregorian Revolution, from Victor II to Eugene III, clearly recalled the last chapter of Biblical history: the early centuries of the Church, during which the very canon of the sacred books had been fixed and developed. The Guelphic leaders, Saint Francis and his followers, as well as Innocent III, lived the passion and cross of Christ and His disciples. Luther, by enthroning the "Predigtamt" of German "Geist" (Spirit) as the controlling power of secular government, restored the prophetic office of the times of Elias, John and Jesus. Cromwell's and William's England reinstated the Judges function and the divine voice of public spirit which had ruled Israel before the Kingdom of David. France went in for the period before the age of revelations-natural man, the God of nature and the rights of Adam before the Fall. And Russia and we contemporaries of Bolshevism delve deep into the pre-adamic and pre-historic forces of labour, sex, youth, primitive tribes and clans, hormones and vitamines."

"This exact sequence, an inverted Biblical chronicle from 300 A. D. back to the first days of life on earth, was traced by revolutionaries who thought themselves completely free, independent and original, and who violently opposed the terms and slogans of every other revolution, preceding or following. Yet they were all under the invincible spell of "One Universal Language for all Mankind." The vigor of this epic unity, binding the national revolutions together, was tested to the utmost by our investigation of the American vocabulary. Half-way between the English and the French, America might not have shared in this strange Biblical retrogression. But this was not so at all. We found in the pamphlets and sermons of the War of Independence the figures of Noah and his sons symbolizing the new cradle of nations in these United States! Noah, Shem, Ham and Japhet, taking their places exactly between the Puritan Judges of Israel and the Rousseauist "Adam," bear witness to the unity of "language" throughout the Christian era, in spite of all national languages. Regeneration of Language would be no faulty name for the due process of Revolution. This process was the means of survival during the sixth day of creation." [96]

Rosenstock-Huessy discloses a backward traveling through the text of the Bible to move forward through history. With the coming of Christ, there is a renewal of the past, not as an interest in antiquities, but a renewal of the past as an unfulfilled promise. It is a kind of updating of the theology of the Church father, Irenaeus, with his doctrine of "recapitulation." All things, all times, all places, all forms of humanity, are recapitulated and renewed in Jesus Christ.[97] Jürgen Moltmann, who as a theologian, comes to an analogous position, says:

"It will no longer be possible to regard the past only archaeologically and take it merely as the origin of the particular future. All history is full of possibilities-possibilities that have been profited by and not profited by, seized and blocked. In this perspective it appears full of interrupted possibilities, lost beginnings, arrested onsets upon the future. Past ages will thus have to be

---

96 Rosenstock-Huessy, E. (1938, reprinted 1969). Out of Revolution; Autobiography of Western Man. Norwich, VT., Argo Books. pp. 738-739

97 "God's saving plan, 'the mystery of his will' (cf. Eph 1: 9) for every creature, is described in the Letter to the Ephesians with a distinctive term: to 'recapitulate' all things in heaven and on earth in Christ (Eph 1: 10). The image could also refer to the roller around which was wrapped the parchment or papyrus scroll of the volume with a written text: Christ gives a single meaning to all the syllables, words and works of creation and history.

"The first person to take up this theme of 'recapitulation' and develop it in a marvelous way was St Irenaeus of Lyons, a great second-century Father of the Church. Against any fragmentation of salvation history, against any division of the Old and New Covenants, against any dispersion of God's revelation and action, Irenaeus extols the one Lord, Jesus Christ, who in the Incarnation sums up in himself the entire history of salvation, humanity and all creation: 'He, as the eternal King, recapitulates all things in himself' "(Adversus Haereses, III, 21, 9). http://www.vatican.va/holy_father/john_paul_ii/audiences/alph/data/aud20010214en.html

understood from the standpoint of their hopes. They were not the background of the now existing present, but were themselves the present and the front-line towards the future. It is the open future that gives us a common front with earlier ages and a certain contemporaneity, which makes it possible to enter into discussion with them, to criticize and accept them. That is why past positions in history and the traces of vanished hopes can be taken up once more and awakened to new life. The dialectic of past happening and present understanding is always motivated by anticipations of the future and by the question of what makes the future possible. Future is then found in the past and possibilities in what has been. The unfinished and promising character of past ages is borne in mind." [98]

Every step forward to find a new future can only be found by receding more deeply into the past. The future is always created by recreating, by remembering, by establishing renaissances of what has come before. Each step forward happens by going further back and laying hold of the unfulfilled promises of the past. The Western world has moved forward by moving backward through the text of Scripture. It has begun at the end, and moved to the beginning. Rosenstock-Huessy claims this is the autobiography of Western man.[99]

---

[98]　Jürgen Moltmann, Theology of Hope; on the ground and implications of a Christian eschatology (New York, Harper & Row, 1967) p. 269

[99]　Rosenstock-Huessy's mode of doing history was to examine the calendars, sermons, pamphlets, and other documents of the contemporaries of those he was studying, and to attempt to discover what their own self understanding of who they were, and where they were in time. He was distinctly interested in "autobiography". Part of his excavation of time periods was to attempt to understand where contemporaries in any given era identified themselves in the text of the narrative of Scripture.

Rosenstock-Huessy's synopsis tells us where we have been, how we have gotten here and where we are going. It is not arbitrary that we have reached the place of the city being central to all we do. In this we find that as Christian history moves forward it begins at the end of the Bible and then moves backward through the Bible.

It also needs to be noted that the continuing presence of the Christian voice as something is established in the Christian world never disappears. It may recede from view, it may become more or less important, but it can be recalled and can reassert its presence and its importance as history moves forward. Institutions that develop in the Christian world become very complex and are constructed of what might be termed layers, with layer upon layer. Hence, the Christian world and the Christian soul become very complex. A psycho-analysis of modern man yields a far more complex soul than the soul of a thousand, or two thousand, or three thousand years ago. Just as Israel has been so troublesome to the digestive system of the world, and appears to be indestructible, because God has made an Everlasting Covenant with these people, so the Christian world likewise becomes indestructible for the same reason. Christian peoples seem never to disappear. The Poles, the Irish, the Estonians simply refuse to disappear or finally assimilate with any other people. And the contributions of any time or place in the Christian world have the

---

Hence, we begin in the early medieval period with the Last Judgment, and find that the Soviets and the free democracies of the 20th Century identified with the "Tohu and Bohu" of Genesis 1:3. This constituted an entire move backward through the narrative of the Bible.

Rosenstock-Huessy, E. (1938, reprinted 1969). *Out of Revolution*; Autobiography of Western Man. Norwich, VT., Argo Books. pp. 738-739

characterization of becoming common property.[100] It is arguable that the Classical world's continuing influence is a continuing influence because the Classical world was inherited by the Church, and it was thus both preserved and transformed. If it had not been for the Christian inheritance of even the most important thinkers of the Classical world, one wonders how enduring even Plato and Aristotle would have been, or how lasting the influence of Roman jurisprudence and administrative skill might have been.[101] It may be that as Christianity moves into the oldest civilizations of Asia and progressively leavens the African Continent that large elements of the great ancient Eastern civilizations and tribal traditions may be reinvigorated in a similar way.

THE UNIVERSITY: A CHRISTIAN INVENTION

A parallel question to be examined is how has the university developed in each of the later periods that Rosenstock-Huessy unveils for us? This is relevant because the university along with the nation state is one of the two great institutions that have developed in western history, and every great city has at least one university. That university will represent much of the ethos of the city, and university renewal is one of the greatest needs of our time. My city is a university town and is dominated by it. A number of

---

100 Rosenstock-Huessy, E. (1938, reprinted 1969). *Out of Revolution; Autobiography of Western Man*. Norwich, VT., Argo Books. p. 621

101 Bonhoeffer argued this in his essay "Ethics as Formation." Bonhoeffer, D. (1965). *Ethics*. New York, Macmillan. pp. 88-109

my most important contacts have been with the university. Rosenstock-Huessy's insights apply to the university, and what was said of layers before are also applicable to the university. Each layer is still there, one built on another, some elements receding and some others dominating, even as new elements are added through time.

Here are the revolutions:

THE PAPAL REVOLUTION

Hildebrand, or Gregory VII (1015-1085), inaugurated the first Christian political revolution in the western world. He was the first Pope to claim to be "the universal pastor of the church."[102] This is what made the creation of the state in the Western world a possibility. It was under the shelter of the papacy that the monarchs of what would be Europe were able to take shelter and grow up together peacefully enough that neighbor states of Christendom could emerge.[103]

The early medieval world found itself in the biblical narrative of the Last Judgment as seen in Dante's Divine Comedy. The Pope (and the Emperor) identified themselves as judges who viewed the world from the end of time.[104] They were an eschatological appearance. This is significant because history to this time had been experienced as cyclical. With the introduction of the end of time, there is an escape from the pagan cycle, and the linear enters

---

102 Rosenstock-Huessy, E. (1938, reprinted 1969). *Out of Revolution; Autobiography of Western Man*. Norwich, VT., Argo Books. p. 534

103 Ibid. pp. 516-519

104 Ibid. , pp. 499-515

history. History as a linear possibility, first disclosed in the Bible, and then unveiled by Augustine, could now begin to be experienced as such. The emphasis on the Last Judgment might appear to limit history as a possibility if the end is imminent. However, the Papacy elongated time with its understanding of the anti-Christ. The end could not come until the anti-Christ appeared. But the anti-Christ could not appear as long as the papacy was vigilant, because the Pope was the guard against his appearance. He could not come if the Pope was on the watch.[105] It was under this shelter that the monarchies could begin to develop.

THE GREAT PREACHING ORDERS

The Franciscans lived wholly in the Gospels and initiated the imitation of Christ and found its consummation in the stigmata. This issued in the only book that Protestants and Catholics have shared since the time of the Reformation: Thomas a Kempis's *The Imitation of Christ*. It was in the era of the Franciscans that city life began to re-conquer Europe. The Dominicans as well as the Franciscans re-inspired the world as great preaching orders. The Renaissance, which is commonly regarded as a great sunrise, was in fact a terrible period when the Church almost collapsed, and the world was falling into what might anachronistically be termed Fascism. It was a great sunset on the period that was begun, two centuries earlier, under the inspiration of these orders.[106]

---

105 Ibid. pp. 552-561

106 Rosenstock-Huessy, E. (1938, reprinted 1969). *Out of Revolution; Autobiography of Western Man*. Norwich, VT., Argo Books. Pp. 577-578, 699ff

The ancient world sought as its end permanence and immutability. The Egyptian Pyramid is a fitting symbol of most of the ancient world's idea of perfection. The perfect would be created, kept and never changed. Plutarch's Lives[107] are not biographies in any modern sense; they are pictures of men who have, as heroes, achieved god-like status and are nearer to being Platonic ideals walking on earth than anything like personalities in the modern sense.[108] The Greek City State and the Roman Empire sought timeless

---

"Actually, the time between 1450 and 1517 is one of the darkest and ugliest hours of the past. The growth of cities ceased all over Europe… petty tyrants destroyed the foundations of local rights. The Church nearly collapsed under the disillusionments of the universal councils and the wars against the Hussites…"

107 Plutarch, A. H. Clough, et al. (1932). The lives of the noble Grecians and Romans. New York, Modern Library.

108 "But more clearly, perhaps, than anywhere else, it comes out in the familiar Parallel Lives. To examine the technique of these biographies is to see that they are each and all constructed in terms of precisely the same concepts. Plutarch thus selects various 'typical' figures of Greek and Roman history in order to depict them as examples of classical character and achievement. The figures depicted are truly representative; but they attain that quality only because the excellences they enshrine belong to an ideal order, which is, ex hypothesi, independent of the flux." Cochrane, C. N. (1957). *Christianity and Classical Culture.* New York, Oxford University Press. p. 169
"It is indeed a suggestive truth [in the light of Augustine's Confessions] that, in more than a thousand years of literary history, the Graeco-Roman world had failed to produce anything which might justly be called a personal record. In this sense, Augustine was perhaps anticipated by the emperor Marcus Aurelius. But the differences between the *Confessions* and the *Meditations* are not less remarkable than the resemblance between them. ...Such differences are far from accidental; they point to the gulf which separates the mentality of the classical from that of the Christian humanist. The former is concerned never to expose a weakness, remembering that it is his business to exemplify as far as possible the conventional type of excellence enshrined in the heroic ideal. The latter is content to defy every canon of Classicism in order merely to bear witness to the truth." Cochrane, C. N. (1957). *Christianity and Classical Culture.* New York, Oxford University Press. p. 386-387

perfection that was beyond change. There was incapacity to cope with time and change in the real world as it was.[109] Augustine's theology could and did deal with change and gave the Christians a leg up in dealing with the collapsing world.[110]

The university was a Christian invention that emerged in the 12th century, that enabled the world to deal with the sense of continual newness that was coming into the world through the Christian revelation. The University of

---

109 Ibid. p. 129, 132

"Our concern is rather with a vicious ideology and with the disastrous consequences of its acceptance by those who were invested with the purple. This we have already tried to describe as the classical ideology of power.

"We have observed how this ideology, erected upon the complementary concepts of virtue and fortune, had attained its apotheosis at Rome in the person of Augustus. Upon his successors it imposed a nemesis from which there could be no escape." Cochrane, C. N. (1957). *Christianity and Classical Culture*. New York, Oxford University Press.   p. 129

"These developments, however striking, serve merely to throw into greater relief the position of the emperor himself as representative and exemplar of the Augustan order. In this capacity there was imposed upon him as perhaps his chief obligation the duty of conformity to a type struck in the mint of the founder; and from this type, even the slightest deviation was abhorrent. Accordingly, the last thing either expected or desired of a Roman emperor was that he should be himself." Cochrane, C. N. (1957). *Christianity and Classical Culture*. New York, Oxford University Press. p. 132

110 Ibid. chapter xi, "Nostra Philosophia", pp. 399-455

"At the same time, Augustinianism emerges, not as a conglomerate of indiscriminate borrowings, but as a mature philosophy which seeks to do justice to all aspects of experience and, in particular, to overcome the apparent discrepancy between the demands of order and those of process, i.e. between the so-called Apolline and Dionysiac elements of life. It thus provides the basis for a synthesis which, whatever may be thought of its claim to finality, serves at least to meet the legitimate aspiration of Classicism for a principle of order; while, in its vision of process and of the goal to which it moves, it discloses worlds to which Classicism, from the limitations of its outlook, remains inevitably blind." Cochrane, C. N. (1957). *Christianity and Classical Culture*. New York, Oxford University Press. p. 400

Paris and Bologna were the first universities. A university is several colleges, often studying the same disciplines but from different perspectives. In Paris, Bonaventure (a Franciscan) and Aquinas (a Dominican) both lectured on theological loci from their own vantage points and students were to listen to both sides debate the issues. Aquinas was broadly an Aristotelian and Bonaventure a Platonist.[111]

This was no longer a world of endless repetition, a cyclical world, but a world of linear development. How does the world cope with difference and newness in some way other than war and banishment? In the ancient world, if Aristotle disagreed with his teacher, Plato, then he had to leave and form his own academy. Now, one is to love one's intellectual enemy under the Christian economy.[112] The university was part of the elongation of history that existed in the time of Western man living with intense consciousness of The Last Judgment.

---

111 Rosenstock-Huessy, E. (1994). *Circulation of Thought* - 1954.(17_15-17) April 28, 1954

112 Ibid.(16-18) April 16, 1954 "...you have said that the university of Plato was a university. No, gentlemen, it was an academy. Plato did not believe in the Augustinian "in *(dubiis) libertas; in (necessariis) unitas.*" He only believed in *unitas,* The calendar of the laws of Plato is an ironclad calendar. You can't get out of it. He would have condemned Socrates a second time to die, if his laws had ever prevailed in his best city. Plato is not a university founder.

"The Plato's school, the academy, and the...higher schools of the Western world are different, to say the least. The principle of the medieval school is: there must be at least two teachers of opposite views on the same topic. In Greece, if you taught differently from Plato, you had to found your own school, the Stoa, or the peripatetic school of Aristotle. You could not stay in the same school. It was impossible to think that one and the same student would be examined by people who held opposite views on--on the doubtful subjects. Such freedom was not known in Greece. This freedom is the --discovery of the Middle Ages..."

THE LUTHERAN REFORMATION

Luther posted the 95 Thesis in 1517 and thereby prompted the next great revolution. Luther appeared as the representative of Paul and the Pauline doctrine. However, Paul was the great anti-type of the Old Testament prophet. The Hebrew prophet spoke to the king. He both instructed and warned him. Paul is always ultimately moving toward Rome, and his final calling is to speak to the Caesar. All through the book of Acts, Paul is constantly speaking to magistrates and thus begins to fulfill the prophesy of Jesus, "They will drag you before kings and magistrates, where you will offer witness to me...." Luther thus represents the Old Testament prophets who speak to kings and magistrates, at one point offering to give his protection to Fredrick when Fredrick again offered him his protection.[113]

Now, the papacy claimed that the end could not come as long as the papacy was doing its job and protecting the world against the anti-Christ. But Luther brought the world to an end when he announced that indeed the anti-Christ had appeared, and the anti-Christ was the Pope himself. Each revolution brings the world to an end and begins it all over again. Luther brought this end and the world began again.[114] A sense of the End of the World and of apocalyptic judgment have since become an essential element in all of Christianized civilization.[115]

---

113 Ibid. p. 389

114 Ibid. pp. 556,

115 It is important to remember that usually the word translated "world" in the New Testament has reference not to space, but to time. Hence, Hebrew 1:2 tells us that "He (Jesus) made the *worlds*...." it is using the word aeons (which means "ages" or "times"). Every revolution brings a new age into

The university was greatly perfected under the German Reformation. Lutheranism was the foundation of all the German universities, and the professor occupied the role of the prophet. Hegel and his philosophical compatriots, were secularized Luthers. "These philosophers-Lessing, Herder, Fitchte, Schelling, Hegel, Feuerbach, Nietzsche-and their lesser collegues, Fries, Krause, Natorp, etc., were descendents of parsons or former theologians themselves and clung to the universality of the theology they inherited.... It is enough to say that they all sacrificed the letter of their theology to save the spirit of the Reformation for an enlightened world. Through their efforts the Lutheran gospel of the living spirit became the 'deutscher Geist.' This much abused phrase is not a nationalistic conception at all. It is the translation of the Holy Ghost into philosophical terms, adapted to the corrupted world which followed the French Revolution-or as Schleirmacher, the theological exponent of the group, called it, an exhortation addressed to the 'Gegildete' among those who disdained religion."[116] This great achievement

being, and the end of a previous age. Hence, we pass from world to world by means of "The Day of the Lord…." by means of judgment. When eschatology is forgotten, it is re-invoked by the godless. Rosenstock-Huessy contends that Nietzsche's philosophy once again conjured up eschatology, which the respectable had endeavored to forget. And, that when France fell to the Nazis in a day, it was a reminder that the world will end. If eschatology is forgotten, it is brought back against the will of those who are the keepers of current fashions. It cannot be eradicated in the Christian era. Marx's entire philosophy was a re-introduction of eschatology, showing that secular prophets will remember what the church endeavors to forget. Rosenstock-Huessy, E. (1947). *The Christian Future : or the Modern Mind Outrun*. London, S.C.M. Press. p. 69-70

116 Rosenstock-Huessy, E. (1938, reprinted 1969). Out of Revolution; Autobiography of Western Man. Norwich, VT., Argo Books. (p. 414-415)
The voice of the prophet speaking to the kings of Israel, the voice of Paul speaking before the governors of Rome, was made a public institution of the German nation when Luther offered Frederick his protection. P.

was severely compromised under the Nazis.[117]

CROMWELL'S ENGLAND

Cromwell by becoming Lord Protectorate in 1644 inaugurated the next great revolution. Cromwell and his Roundheads committed regicide, and by committing this crime, they radicalized what Luther had done. Luther called the Church to prophesy to the king. Cromwell eliminated the king and thus moved behind the prophets and the kings in the Bible to the time of the Judges.[118]

Cambridge was the Puritan university. A very high percentage of early natural scientists were Calvinistic and Puritan in sympathy.[119] The strong doctrine of creation

---

389 The public in Germany thought of the universities as keepers of the nations conscience. p 398

117 Rosenstock-Huessy, E. (1938, reprinted 1969). *Out of Revolution; Autobiography of Western Man*. Norwich, VT., Argo Books.
The system of religious parties to which the universities were central has been overruled in Germany today. Hitler is a pre-Reformation type, by race, education and character. He is immune to the last four centuries of German history. He is neither a Protestant nor an academic person nor a civil servant nor an army officer. P. 442-443

118 Ibid. p. 331-332

119 "It's easy to document the religious values and beliefs of many English scientists of this period. John Ray (1627-1705), the great biologist, told a friend that time spent investigating nature was well used: "What time you have to spare you will do well to spend, as you are doing, in the inquisition and contemplation of the works of God and nature." Forty-two of the 68 founding members of the Royal Society (England's premier scientific organization) for which their religious background is known were Puritans. Since the English population was mostly mainstream Anglican in belief, the high proportion of Puritans in it implies their values encouraged scientific endeavors. Sir Robert Moray, Sir William Petty, Robert Boyle, John Wilkins, John Wallis, and Jonathan Goddard were all prominent leaders of the Royal Society—and all Puritans."
Snow, E. V. *Christianity: A Cause of Modern Science*, Impact # 298.

and of the decree of a sovereign God made possible the discovery of God's mind by man's mind. The English professor was an extension of the landed gentry. He was in part a creation of Cromwell.[120]

British repression is also the fruit of Cromwell. Cromwell is the Oedipus of the English speaking peoples. In committing regicide, he "murdered his father" and came close to marrying his mother, the British people. He only avoided this by remaining the Lord Protector and refusing to become a king. The result was Britain had to hide the source of her modern greatness in her domination of the seas and the creation of an empire on which the sun never set. It was Cromwell who laid all of the foundations for this, but this could not be acknowledged.[121] Psycho-analysis had to be invented in Vienna to save the English from their Oedipal repressions.

THE AMERICAN REVOLUTION

The American Revolution identified itself with the time of Noah. America was perceived as a virgin continent. The ships of the old world landed in a new world that was unoccupied, just as Noah's ark landed on a completely new and virgin world. America was natural, and there was a distinctive emphasis on the natural and natural law as inheritors of the Noahic Covenant.[122]

---

120 Rosenstock-Huessy, E. (1938, reprinted 1969). Out of Revolution; Autobiography of Western Man. Norwich, VT., Argo Books. pp. 322-332

121 Rosenstock-Huessy, E. (1938, reprinted 1969). *Out of Revolution; Autobiography of Western Man.* Norwich, VT., Argo Books. Pp. 257-358

122 Ibid. pp. 675, 678-686, 711, 738-739

The American land grant college was created to carve out the natural to form a new world.[123] This is America's one original contribution to the university. Rosenstock-Huessy says, "In France, nature is a relief from an aristocratic civilization; in the colonies, nature is attacked day after day by a body of pioneering individuals, who must stick to the facts and have no time for abstract ideas. In a virgin country, Nature is not lazy. She threatens you with annihilation if you do not move faster than she does." And enhancing the citizen's ability to do this is the purpose of the land grant institution.[124] Hence, "nature" has a very different meaning in the American context than the French, even though there are analogical similarities.

The American university is not original, but the great inheritor of all of Europe. Allan Bloom said of his teaching experience that the one book that was the American book was the Bible, and after that America does not have a national literature like the nations of Europe, but is the

---

123 A land-grant college or university is an institution that has been designated by its state legislature or Congress to receive the benefits of the Morrill Acts of 1862 and 1890. The original mission of these institutions, as set forth in the first Morrill Act, was to teach agriculture, military tactics, and the mechanic arts as well as classical studies so that members of the working classes could obtain a liberal, practical education.

A key component of the land-grant system is the agricultural experiment station program created by the Hatch Act of 1887. The Hatch Act authorized direct payment of federal grant funds to each state to establish an agricultural experiment station in connection with the land-grant institution there. Segregated Southern states came to be known as "the 1890 land-grants." The 29 Native American tribal colleges are sometimes called the "1994 land-grants."

124 Rosenstock-Huessy, E. (1938, reprinted 1969). *Out of Revolution; Autobiography of Western Man.* Norwich, VT., Argo Books. p. 659

inheritor of all of Western literature.[125] America is the
absorber of all that came before her in the Europe she left
behind.

THE FRENCH REVOLUTION

The French identified themselves with the unfallen
Adam in the Garden. They would recreate a garden paradise
by means of unfallen reason. "France went in for the period
before the age of revelations-natural man, the God of nature
and the rights of Adam before the Fall."[126]

The contribution of the French Enlightenment is the
ethos of one of the deepest and most pervasive layers of
the modern university. The dogma of the autonomy of
reason has almost entirely eclipsed the earlier foundation
of the university in revelation. Theology as the Queen of

---

125 Bloom, A. D. (1987). *The closing of the American mind.* New York, Simon
and Schuster. p. 47-61

126 Ibid. p. 739, also see p. 198

It should also be noted that the French Revolution identified itself as a
revolution in opposition to Christianity. This is significant. Part of what
this means is that even when a part of the world that is christianized
attempts to break away from the Kingdom of God, it is still defined
by the Kingdom of God. The French Revolution, in concert with other
anti-Christian movements and moments in Western Civilization, are still
defined by what they are against. This would be true of the Renaissance,
and the Enlightenment, and of seminal figures like Nietzsche and Marx.
Rosenstock-Huessy said this about the anti-Christian character of the
Renaissance: "The Renaissance though much of its content was pagan,
was thus in the long view an event inside Christianity, begun by sparks
ignited in a common plight of Eastern and Western Christendom."
Rosenstock-Huessy's contention is that the Renaissance was the result
of aiming at the reunion of the Eastern and Western Church and failing,
but the world instead finding a new unity that healed the wound of
the Church, the world found a new unity in science and mathematics
founded in Plato and a renewal of the Platonic academy.

Every revolution likewise is founded deeply in the Christian era, even if it
is rebelling against it.

the Sciences and the chief of all disciplines was replaced almost entirely by a philosophy of autonomous reason and humanistic literature. Rosenstock-Huessy says this in regard to the French nation-state and, consequently, the French university (which came to represent all universities in the western world).

"The modern 'idea' of a nation, like the other 'ideas' we have surveyed, is the result of a purifying process. The old concept of nation had been that of a geographical subdivision within the Church. A nation was a group of scholars, doctors and princes at one of the Christian Councils. At the great councils of the fifteenth century the French nation was led by the University of Paris.

"Now, in the eighteenth century, the nation had to be organized outside the Church, outside Christianity, in the natural world: the doctors of theology were replaced by the writers and expounders of philosophy, and the estates of France-King, clergy, nobility-by the Freemasons of reason. These elements formed the 'nation.' Wherever modern nationalism in Europe succeeded in founding a nation state within natural borders, literature and the lodge were at its back. The modern nation is therefore not a product of nature but of literature, not a body of mere inhabitants but of listeners and readers of modern philosophy and science."[127]

The home of the philosophy of autonomous reason and of humanistic literature that does not need God is this layer of the university, created out of the womb of the French

---

127 Rosenstock-Huessy, E. (1938, reprinted 1969). *Out of Revolution; Autobiography of Western Man*. Norwich, VT., Argo Books.
　　p. 198-199

Enlightenment and Revolution.

THE RUSSIAN REVOLUTION

The Soviets identified themselves with "the formless and the void" of Genesis 1:2. They identified with the chaos. The whole of the 20th century has identified with the chaos and has lived in the great hope that a dip into the chaos by means of revolution would rejuvenate the world.[128]

One is struck at the outset by the fact that to the Bolshevik mind revolution is an end and not a means. The term is given a queer sense of permanence. This concept of a continuous never-ending state of affairs to be called "perpetual revolution" certainly is cumbersome for any liberal mind. However, all post war revolutionaries agree in the new terminology. Hitler and Mussolini, as much as Stalin, are attemping today to bring about a complete change in our political vision. They are proclaiming "revolution" to be the only decent political status for human beings. Intervals of mere legal and peaceful order are branded as treason against the true concept of life. Darwin's "struggle for existence" is transformed by these political dogmatists into the new term, "continuous revolution." Order, stability, peace, security are dethroned. They are inexcusable symbols of darkness and cowardice....

> Bolshevism is less concerned with showing its true faith than it is with tearing off the mask of the French Revolution worn by the governing class. Its perpetual revolution goes against a temporary revolution. With the French it is anti-

---

128 Ibid. pp. 109,112, 738-739 Rushdoony, R. J. (1965). *The Religion of Revolution*. Victoria, Texas, Trinity Episcopal Church.

bourgeois, anti-liberal, anti-democratic, anti-national. It is the dissolution of the existing order, the only paradox being that it is its perpetual dissolution. A perpetual dissolution is a contradiction in terms. But this contradiction is at the root of Bolshevism.... Because the proletarian is the negation of the bourgeois his creed begins with nihil and the dissolution of Family, State, Law, Art, and Religion is its revolutionary desire.[129]

The Russian Revolution of 1917 has given us the last layer of the university. The enthronement of chaos, the lifting up of Genesis 1:2 explains much about the modern university. The pervasive Leftism of the university is the excrescence of revolutionary Marxism. And the sciences have all sought to ground themselves in the chaos of Darwinism and populist understandings of Quantum Mechanics and Relativity. The university is now almost without rudder or orientation. One cannot ground either a civilization or learning on chaos for very long. It is only if one remembers that the first half of Genesis 1:2 recounts that the chaos (the tohu and the bohu) is followed by hovering of the Spirit of God, Who authors the creation week and creates a new world, that any newness can come of this. But modernity comes to its own end by assiduously striving to forget the second half of the second verse of Genesis.[130]

129 Rosenstock-Huessy, E. (1938, reprinted 1969). *Out of Revolution; Autobiography of Western Man.* Norwich, VT., Argo Books. p. 111-112

130 "The university may have come near to its death when Heidegger joined the German people-especially the youngest part of that people, which he said had already made an irreversible commitment to the future-and put philosophy at the service of German culture. If I am right in believing that Heidegger's teachings are the most powerful intellectual force in our times, then the crisis of the German university, which everyone saw, is the crisis of the university everywhere." Bloom, A. D. (1987). *The closing of the American mind.* New York, Simon and Schuster. p. 311-312

CHAOS, REGRESSION AND CONTROL

The cult of the child is upon us. To quote Eugen Rosenstock-Huessy:

"The longing to dance, behave, forget, dream like a child is felt increasingly. The stages of the first twenty years of a man's life, which in former days were treated as steps preparatory for old age, are changing before our eyes as into ends in themselves…. this cult of childishness is spreading everywhere…."[131]

The oddity is that in fact, increasingly, we live in a world of the old. Marriage in what we call the First World is rarer, and, when it happens, it is more often sterile. Birthrates are dropping, but the impulse is to swim against the stream.

Bloom saw the undermining and deconstructing of the American university in the "60s" as a result of the afterglow of all of the same ideas emanating from German irrationalism that dominated the Weimar Republic in the twenties and early thirties, as coming to fruition in America at that time. He goes on to say," What happened to the universities in Germany in the thirties is what has happened and is happening everywhere. The essence of it all is not social, political, psychological, or economic, but philosophic." Ibid p. 312. For Bloom, the answer is in a renewed reflection on the high points of Greek thought in Plato and Aristotle, but particularly in Socrates, who was the first martyr for the rights of thought against the chaos of the populace. He says, "A serious argument about what is most profoundly modern leads inevitably to the conclusion that study of the problem of Socrates is the one thing most needful. It is Socrates who made Nietzsche and Heidegger look to the pre-Socratics. For the first time in four hundred years, it seems possible and imperative to begin all over again, to try to figure out what Plato was talking about, because it might be the best thing available." Ibid p. 310. The writer would argue that renewed reflection on Socrates as the "martyr of thought" can only possibly be fruitful inside the larger parameters of the death and resurrection of Christ. The university is an institution created inside the Christian era ("the age of ages"), and it is impossible apart from that.

131 Rosenstock-Huessy, E. (1938, reprinted 1969). *Out of Revolution; Autobiography of Western Man.* Norwich, VT., Argo Books. p. 717

As we age, as we increasingly do not have either children or grandchildren, we become children ourselves. The ideal of an aging world is to be transformed into the completely immature.

The evidences are everywhere for us to see. On most evenings, I see on television advertisements for the latest reality shows one is "She's Got the Look" in which aging and middle aged women (one of them boasting that she is fifty) compete for a chance to be a fashion model, a career that usually ends before a young lady is in her middle twenties.[132]

Dostoyevsky foresaw this very clearly. One of his most prophetic novels was titled *The Adolescent.*[133] He foresaw that youthful rebellion, youthful arrogance, was the future of Russia and that the results would be terrible indeed.

One has the sense that the ideal of life is to be about

132 This is precisely the opposite of the early medieval period when old age was emphasized, because there were so few of the old, and the world was populated almost exclusively by the young. Ibid. P 519
'The Triumph of Old Age

'The aescetic monk on the papal throne spoke still from the beyond. At his "conversion" a monk was buried in symbolical forms; he handed over his life, his property, his family, to his patron. He died in every sense. He lived and anticipated a spiritual world.

'"Civil death" or monastic death is a legal term which describes the consequences of the monastic profession. Gregory VII manifested the monk's spiritual world of after-death as a cradle of government. Ancestoral wisdom from beyond the grave was introduced into a world threatened by child mortality, juvenile leadership, and the rare survival of people past middle age. Today man's life spiral so often reaches the third circle, from sixty to ninety years, that this age is not especially emphasized as a basis for a certain attitude toward government. At that time the tremendous lack of older men made it advisable to specialize in the features of old age, of the non-agenarian with his natural resignation and renouncement. The monk's existence is an artificial substitute for the man who has waived all his claim because of age.'

133 Dostoyevsky, F. (1971). *The Adolescent.* Garden City, N.Y.,, Doubleday.

sixteen, to wear short pants, to carry a skateboard and to wear a baseball cap backwards. The cult of the youth has entered the Church like a tsunami. Everywhere we have the liturgy of the adolescent. A large number of churches are sure that all of the future is to be found in transforming worship into what one is tempted to see as a giant junior high youth group, with adolescent songs and preaching designed to speak to all of the problems of adolescents. To be adult is no longer the ideal or even conceived of as a possibility.

Rosenstock-Huessy's scheme of history emphasizes that we have arrived at the place of chaos. Genesis 1:2 is the place of "the formless and the void." We have regressed to the very beginning of the world, to the childhood of the world.[134]

The dominant political expressions of the 20th century were all expressions of the youth swimming in chaos. Fascism and Communism were the politics of violent revolution. Beyond that, even the hard sciences have sought a metaphysic that is a metaphysic of chaos. Darwinism, by forgetting the second half of the second verse of Genesis, ironically, is a recapturing of the metaphysics of the ancient world. It is a metaphysic of chaos that believes that order can miraculously emerge out the chaos. It is an updating of the Babylonian story of Marduk emerging (no one knows how) from water, the ancient symbol of chaos.

I have found universally with contemporary leaders that they know that they are up against the irresponsible, the childish, but often at the same time participate in a

---

134 Rosenstock-Huessy, E. (1938, reprinted 1969). *Out of Revolution; Autobiography of Western Man.* Norwich, VT., Argo Books. p. 739

idealization of youthfulness. It bears mentioning that we stand in exactly the opposite place from the ancient world in regard to where we look for direction (in our deep lack of orientation). The ancient world universally revered what came before, the past, the traditions of the elders. Jesus' war with the Pharisees and Sadducees was with their reverencing the traditions of the elders over the Word of God. Now everything is for the children. The Word of God is buried not in tradition and what came before, but in an inchoate and vague future. But this is actually only modern, upside down Phariseeism. God's Word is subverted for the future, which is essentially contentless or only an enhancement of the present. It is not really different, or new or a development. Just as ancient Phariseeism could only reproduce what was stale, so now seeking direction purely in youth and a vague future can only do the same.

It is also the case that chaos calls forth it's opposite. Since chaos is intolerable and cannot be lived with for very long, it calls up its opposite, and its opposite may be as terrible and as intolerable as the chaos itself. Its opposite is absolute control. Politically, it expresses itself in tyranny and totalitarianism. Scientifically and metaphysically, it expresses itself in iron determinism. Hence, we have dialectic with which most of the 20th century struggled. It is the dialectic of chaos and tyranny, or chaos and determinism.[135]

It is also the case that the two earliest human configurations have come to be co-terminus. Those are tribalism and empire. The tribal man lives closer to the

---

135 Dooyeweerd, H. (1969). *A New Critique of Theoretical Thought*. Philidelphia, Presbyterian and Reformed Publishing Company. Vol. 1, pp. 403-495

primitive chaos and in almost a perfect anarchy. The empire is the place of complete control and even tyranny. Today we see the American or African tribal identity being called up in the midst of a world wide global empire.

GLOBAL ECONOMY AND NEO-TRIBALISM

Rosenstock-Huessy said as long ago as his publication of *Out of Revolution* that the next move for humanity was the rise of both a global economy and neo-tribalism. In 1938 he said this:

"In the future, many buried instincts will have to be revived in the white man[136] if he is really to survive in this age of "childhood regained" into which a senile world is plunging. Here senility is no metaphor. In this world of one child families, old age pensions, birth control and the abolition of illness, youth is in a minority, with its proper contribution neglected, as was old age a thousand years ago. Gregorian Papacy was then the cure for too much clannishness and tribalism. Today clannishness and primitivism may be recalled to life, to restore the balance of a senile world in which there are three adults to one child. The longing to dance, behave, forget, dream like a child is felt increasingly. The stages of the first twenty years of a man's life, which in former days were treated as steps prepatory for old age, are changing before our eyes as into ends in themselves. Though this cult of childishness is spreading everywhere, Germany, removing its harness of paternalism in a kind of orgy, is anticipating the tribalism of the next

---

136 Rosenstock-Huessy was lecturing in the 1950s and seems here to mean "western man."

three hundred years. They especially long to return to the "archetypes" of childhood and primordial dawn, to rites of initiation and pagan sacrifice because Germans crave a fountain of youth. But until the economic unity of the world is established, the return to dream states would prove fatal. These dream states are admissible only as an antidote, in the education of the masses in the national sectors of the globe."

"Before any tribe or group can sacrifice reason to the unreal myth and magic of pre-history, its food and shelter must be guaranteed by the peaceful world-wide organization of production. Nazism is premature; it cannot coexist with the potentiality of war. Frightened by the proletarian Revolution, the Nazis are attempting a "classless nation," a solution which lies even beyond the Russian society. They are developing the characteristics of the primitive tribes before they can commit themselves to such an adventure. And the professed pacifism hinges upon the fact that the Nazis plan to return into the forests like the Germanic tribes. The Jews, who represent the universal history of mankind, stand in their way. Yet is perhaps only through the Jews that the world may become a playground for tribal primitivism! Possibly the Jews will contribute more than others to that universal organization of production which makes wars impossible and leads in a world-wide economy. This is the necessary presupposition for the revival of primitive archetypes in different sectors of the globe. Since, this revival is interested in buried instincts, it can be neither Christian nor philosophical, in the sense in which the English, American or French Revolutionaries were philosophical or the Roman, Italian, and German were Christian.

"The early stages of human development will be the goal of efforts which will no longer be deliberate or logical revolutions. They will be "Relapses" into instinctive phases of primitive life and "Reproductions" of archetypes. That is why our future evolution will lead to a variety of special reproductions. A relapse toward the dawn of civilizations is opposed to any world-wide generalization. It will be the pride of such a relapse to be anti-universal and limited to a single or social group. Economy will be universal, mythology regional. Every step in the direction of organizing the world's economy will have to be bought off by a great number of tribal reactions."[137]

Rosenstock-Huessy published this nearly eighty years ago. In the meantime, reality has continued to catch up to his prophetic insight. In the last twenty years, Francis Fukayma published *The End of History* in which he announced the final triumph of democratic capitalism, the end of war, the triumph of the rationality of market economics that would render war impossible, because capitalist nations do not go to war with other nations that are potential markets.[138] Then we saw the publication of several ground breaking articles in "Atlantic Monthly" by Robert D. Kaplin, announcing almost the opposite of Fukyama. In a rising tide of barbarism and tribalism that could even potentially sink civilization as we know it, Kaplin announced that we are not one world and universal rational markets may not

---

137 Rosenstock-Huessy, E. (1938, reprinted 1969). *Out of Revolution; Autobiography of Western Man*. Norwich, VT., Argo Books. pp 717-718

138 Francis Fukuyama, *The End of History and the Last Man* (New York; Free Press; Toronto; Maxwell Macmillan Canada; New York; Maxwell Macmillan International, c1992)

be on an unclouded horizon.[139] Samuel Huntington has also published announcing that we have come to a time of the clash of cultures, and there is no overarching unifying series of principles.[140] Stanley Fish says much the same thing as he brilliantly applies the epistemological insights that he gained through years of literary criticism around the poetry and theology of John Milton (there is no neutral or objective stance that any cultural group can occupy to critique other cultural groups).[141] In all of this, Fukuyama is a child of Hegel, and all of the other authors are either knowingly, or unknowingly, children of Nietzsche and his announcement of the end of rationality and the rise of cultures.

In a middle ground, we have seen the publication of several studies on the part of Thomas Friedman that acknowledge the rise of a global economy in what he announces is a flattened playing field, whatever the complexities of that field. And he has thrown into the mix the rising global power of the two Asian giants, China and India.[142]

Hence, in recent years many people have observed one side or the other of the now observable complex of global economy/tribal and neo-tribalism. To my knowledge,

---

139 Robert D. Kaplan, "The Coming Anarchy", The Atlantic Monthly, February, 1994 http://www.theatlantic.com/ideastour/archive/kaplan.mhtlm

140 Samuel P. Huntington, *The Clash of Civilizations And the Remaking of World Order* (New York, Simon and Schuster, c1996)

141 Stanley Fish, *The Trouble With Principle* (Cambridge, Mass., Harvard University Press, 1999)
Stanley Fish, *How Milton Works* (Cambridge, Mass Belnap Press of Harvard University Press, 2001)

142 Thomas L. Friedman, *The World Is Flat: A Brief History of the 21st Century* (New York: Farrar, Straus and Giroux, 2006)

nobody has yet captured the fullness of Rosenstock-Huessy's insight that it will be both at the same time and both acting as anodynes to each other. In most studies, we see the continued idea that one side or the other (global economy as a reproduction of the great ancient empires, or neo-tribalism) will dominate with the other side acting as a hindrance on the other. This makes the picture messy, dangerous and less comprehensible and predictable. One would rather wish for a simple and unhindered picture.[143] Rosenstock-Huessy saw both sides as essential out workings of the further development of the entire race and both sides as being essential.

Nothing in God's world ever disappears. Each people grouping and civilization builds on the next, but even though nothing disappears, new layers are built on old layers, and new ideas, structures, configurations, assume new importance, and old ideas, structures and configurations, recede into the background. The nation state is one of these layers.

It is perfectly clear in the early 21st century that the nation state is not going to disappear. The utter importance

---

143 Thomas Friedman has recently come to grips with the reality of globalism with localism and tribalism functioning at the same time.

Thomas L. Friedman, The Lexus and the Olive Tree (New York, Anchor Books c2000)

"With vivid stories and a set of original terms and concepts, Friedman shows us how to see this new system. He dramatizes the conflict of 'the Lexus and the olive tree' the tension between the globalization system and ancient forces of culture, geography, tradition, and community. He also details the powerful backlash that globalization produces among those who feel brutalized by it, and he spells out what we all need to do to keep this system in balance."

From Thomas Friedman's page on NY Times

http://www.thomasfriedman.com/bookshelf/the-lexus-and-the-olive-tree

of the United States, China, India, Russia and a hundred other nation states continue and will continue to dominate world power and trade structures. And yet a new layer of multi-national corporations and trade agreements effectively transcend the nation state reality in significant ways. The new nerve centers or ganglions are cities. Within these cities we find both phenomena reproduced. The cities are the heart of the faceless global economy and are filled with faceless people who are configuring, or reconfiguring themselves, into neo-tribal groupings, seeking a face and an identity. It may be more important what city I occupy than what nation state houses any given city.

This is the analysis of where we are and may be for a long time, but it is difficult to give any guidance to the leader if all he has to work with are chaos and tyranny or chaos and determinism. We need a new ideal; we need a new telos.

Chapter Six

THE NEW JERUSALEM

I had coffee one morning with the man who at one time was the highest executive officer in my city and at that point held a similar position in another organization. He has become a good friend and is a Christian. I thought he would be a good man to run my thoughts past to see if what I had been thinking was just my fantasizing, or is this a viable possibility in the real world of policy and politics?

How can renewal come? Rosenstock-Huessy says, to paraphrase him, that the nation state has become senile. It is one of the two great institutions of the last 500 years (the university being the other). The growth of the totalitarian state in the 20th century is the sign of senility, just as witch trials were the sign of the senility of the previous era of Medieval Christendom.

The United States is suppose to be a structure of various jurisdictions, with states being the primary jurisdiction outside of the federal government that push back or give counter weight to the nation. This is being challenged with extensive top heavy federalization. There is now polarization, and some states have increasingly become shadows of the federal government and offer little or no contrast, while a few others are asserting some interesting independence.[144] The absorption of the lower by the higher can be seen in the case of California (to pick one state out for illustrative purposes), and it illustrates the vicious circle in which we are caught. California is bankrupt and now is more than happy to sell its pot of stew to simply become, more or less, an appendage to the federal government. California is as bloated a bureaucracy as Washington. There is no contrast or too little to matter.

What if we went down even further and cities became the push back? What if cities began to stand up to the feds (and the states) and just said, "No!"? Could they do that? Is that feasible? What if Jack Kemp's ideas about enterprise zones were adopted by whole municipalities, or clusters of municipalities, and not just applied to depressed and ghettoized segments of cities?[145] The vicious circle is obvious and the absurdity of it is becoming ever clearer. The states are broke and need to be bailed out, and the feds are broke and need to be bailed out too. The feds have the advantage of being able to print money but are just as broke.

---

144 Notably, Texas, Wisconson, and New Jersey, at the time of writing this paper (2014).

145 Jack Kemp (1935-2009) was for many years the Representative to Congress of New York's 31st Congressional District, and he proposed renewing cities through "Enterprise Zones" in which depressed areas in cities are able to offer tax concessions, infra-structure incentives, and reduced regulation to attract investment and development.
    http://www.nytimes.com/2014/04/06/sunday-review/note-to-republicans-channel-jack-kemp.html?_r=0
http://www.newsmax.com/US/detroit-rand-paul-enterprise/2013/12/05/id/540101/
http://townhall.com/columnists/jackkemp/2003/02/25/enterprise_zones_of_choice

The cities, even though many of them are also broke, are the real economic foundation where everything originates and happens. What if they defied the bloated and out of control bureaucracies that hamper them all of the time and declared a measure of autonomy? It would not be withdrawal from the U. S. or the state, but push back. This would be limited revolution sanctioned by lesser magistrates, as Calvin would have called them.

My friend was delighted with the idea and said that in his mind it was feasible. He said he could almost see it. An aide or advisor comes into the White House one day with an announcement that ten cities were doing something like this in concert and the White House saying with astonishment, "Boston, New York, Houston, Denver, Minneapolis, Seattle, Oakland, New York, Miami, Atlanta are going to do what?" And cities could start to get away with it.[146]

He pointed out that city government is comparatively sleek and very responsive. One could see, over the next hundred years, whole islands of renewed city states growing up world wide. It would not be in a vacuum, but a new layer on top of the old, and all of these cities would still have the old connections, but with renewed and differentiated relationships.

The very, very odd thing is that China is already doing this. Shanghai, as a whole city, has been established as essentially an Enterprise Zone in a way similar to what Kemp was stumping for years ago. Tax rates have been

---

146 This would be the Conservative revolutionary corollary to Richard Cloward and Francis Fox Piven's Alinskite proposal: *The Weight of the Poor: A Strategy To End Poverty* http://www.americanthinker.com/2011/08/ cloward-piven_paradise_now.html http://www.discoverthenetworks. org/groupProfile.asp?grpid=7522

dramatically dropped, and certain protections have been given to entrepreneurs, and all is being done to promote enterprise.[147]

If ten mayors from ten major cities declared their cities enterprise zones all at once, just what would the feds and the states do? In a few years, the feds and states would be at city limits with hat in hand.

Here is the shift: what if we began to think of cities as the central human configuration rather than nation states? What if we took seriously the reality that nation states are literally bankrupt, and there is no federal breast to suck on? What if we faced reality and acknowledged that it is in cities that almost all of our economic activity exists, that the feds produce nothing but controls and controls that are far from the realities over which they have authority?

When I have said these things to two chief executives who have been in charge of my city government, in both cases their faces lit up. The last time I met and talked about some of these things with one of them, one of them said that she had just returned from D.C. during the annual "come to Washington with your hands held out to get federal bucks" time. She hates it increasingly and increasingly recognizes the futility of it. The other points out that most cities (there are notable exceptions, the ones most "federalized,") actually have to balance budgets and have to use money efficiently. Both are very open to the

---

147 Recent proposals on the part of Rand Paul are proposing just this. It moves against the absurdity of taxing the cities heavily, and then the feds giving that same money back with federal strings and controls that make effective use of that money impossible. Even a disaster like Detroit has huge sums of money taxed out of it by the federal government, that could far more efficiently be used with local control.

thought that rejuvenation will come from the metropolitan arena. The nation state is bankrupt, and that is true both economically and ideologically.

When things are turned upside-down with cities being recognized as most basic, most essential, and the source of almost all economic production and human sustenance, and states secondary and nation states a third in importance, it changes everything. The nation state still exists, but primarily for national defense and to protect interstate and intra-city commerce, so that trade wars cannot break out. When all of this seems completely sensible, and people who twenty minutes ago were garden variety liberals suddenly start thinking and talking more like what we might call libertarians, something interesting is happening.

At one point I wrote to both of them and sent them a quote from the fifth chapter ("Dumbed Down Taxes") from the book, *The Dark Age Ahead*, by the redoubtable metropolist Jane Jacobs. Her concern in that chapter is just who has the primary power of taxation? The principle of subsidiary and the principle of fiscal accountability say that "government works best… when it is closest to the people it serves," and "that institutions collecting and disbursing taxes work most responsibly when they are transparent to those providing the money."[148]

The cities of the Roman Empire had lost these advantages in the desperate years before the collapse, when the imperial treasury extorted from them as much as it could and disbursed the money for schemes and needs according

---

148 Jane Jacobs, *Dark Age Ahead*, Vintage Books (A Division of Random House), New York, 2004; page 79-80

to its own, frequently crazed priorities. The early medieval cities regained the two principles slowly, in various ways. Some, like London, received royal charters authorizing them to farm (that is, collect) their own taxes. Others, like Hamburg and cities of the Low Countries and northern France, gained subsidiarity and fiscal accountability through the efforts of merchants and citizens united by common interests and then, increasingly, by custom. Many others, like Venice itself, Florence, Bologna and Genoa, achieved subsidiarity and fiscal accountability as by products of their own sovereignty as city states.

Both principles are important but the need for subsidiarity has become especially acute for reasons I shall sketch out later. Yet both subsidiarity and fiscal accountability of public money have almost disappeared from the modern world, as if a cycle is returning to the Roman imperium, rather than to principles that renewed Western culture long after Rome's failure. Today, over almost all the world, major taxes, including those most remunerative and most economically informative, like income taxes based on ability to pay, or those directly reflecting economic expansion, like sales or value-added taxes, are collected either by sovereign governments or by their surrogates, provincial governments. This is true of federal governments like those of the United States, Canada, Mexico and Germany, and of centralized sovereignties like those of England, France, Sweden, and Israel—to name a few of both types. The only exceptions are a few city states like Hong Kong and Singapore and near city states like the Czech Republic (the city state of Prague), Slovakia (the city-state of Bratislava) and Taiwan (the city state of Taipei). Only very minor taxation, such as property taxes, responsive neither to ability to pay nor to economic expansion, is typically permitted to cities.[149]

They were both delighted and thrilled that someone articulated what they have come to feel so deeply. However, the danger is much greater. No administration of any age will ever cede its power easily, voluntarily or without considerable and widespread resistance (even to the point of using police or military power in resistance).

If it were only true that necessity is the mother of invention, we would have political invention on the verge of happening, but since opportunity is actually the mother of invention, this needed political invention hasn't materialized. "The closest things to such events happening in our times are the peaceful separation of Singapore from Malaysia and the peaceful separation of Czechoslovakia into the two sovereignties of the Czech Republic and Slovakia. But in most countries such separation would risk terrorism and warfare, as has happened in Sri Lanka, Cyprus and Chechnya and has been threatened elsewhere in places to numerous to mention.... Dumbed down use of taxes—and the dumbed-down use of powers the taxes make possible— imposes deterioration, and it is surprising how rapidly this can happen once it gets under way...."[150]

We need intelligent revolution on the part of the lower magistrates as Calvin would have called them.

There has been some dreaming on the part of libertarian types of the withdrawal of states from the Union in order to re-establish limited government I think this is a pipe-

149 Ibid, p. 79-80

150 Ibid p. 79-80

dream, but cities being renewed in this way and becoming the real counterweight instead of withdrawing from the nation state is an authentic possibility and is not just a pipe-dream. My friends also think this, who should know about real world possibilities. But this will never happen easily or without considerable resistance.

Edwin Friedman in his *Failure of Nerve* gives these three characteristics of gridlocked systems which have come to characterize our failing era. He outlines them as: "1) an unending treadmill of trying harder, 2) looking for answers rather than reframing questions, and 3) either/or thinking that creates false dilemmas."[151]

Trying to think of how to save our civilization by reforming the nation state has led to these impasses. Liberals want more nation state control, conservatives less. Conservatives are, I believe right, but cannot break out of being essentially negative. Conservatives are against big and remote government, against wasteful, out-of-control spending and against Tower-of-Babel-like central planning that comes from far, far away.[152] This may all be correct, but perhaps sterile. I live in a very progressive city. I know how fixed these debates are and how hopeless. But when one can meet with people from the inside establishment, from inside of government, and turn things on their head and

---

151 Edwin H. Friedman, *A Failure of Nerve,* Seabury Books, New York, 1999. p. 34

152 Probably the best summation of the economic principles conservatives believe in is F.A. Heyek's Road to Serfdom, (University of Chicago Press, Chicago) 1976, c1944. I understand that Daniel Patrick Moynihan used to give away copies of this very commonly to colleagues, and especially Republicans, in order that they might be acquainted with their own heritage. Hayek, by the way, did not identify himself as a conservative, but as an authentic and original liberal.

reframe the questions, one sees that it changes everything.

There is, however, a deeper issue in all of this. Economic theory and policy are not an adequate fulcrum point. We are reframing things as essentially an entire covenant renewal, something as fundamental in the Old Testament of the Bible as a change from the era of the Judges to the era of Monarchy, or Monarchy to the great Empires. The deeper issue is a theological issue of vision. It is a question of typology, of symbolism. This is not secondary because the very being of man and woman is that they are the image of God. Another way of saying this is "man is the symbol of God." Our symbols are the deepest thing about us and in the end entirely control how we think, act and move. The real city in the city is the Church, and the model that would guide everything would not be the Greek city state, but The New Jerusalem. This is the real engine behind anything like this happening. The New Jerusalem as the broad sociological model has never happened before. It also does something to what Daniel Patrick Moynihan was entirely frustrated about. He was amongst the first to recognize the disaster of the collapse of the family and marriage, but he said repeatedly that he had no idea what to do about it.[153] And it is also the case that there are plenty of criticisms of Kemp's Enterprise Zone idea. It does not always work.[154] When it does not work, it is not because it is inadequate as an economic theory. It is inadequate because conservative

153 www.heritage.org/research/lecture/the-collapse-of-marriage-and-the-rise-of-welfare-dependence

154 http://beforeitsnews.com/opinion-conservative/2014/01/enterprise-zones-a-jack-kemp-idea-2787704.html
http://www.thefiscaltimes.com/Columns/2014/01/10/Enterprise-Zones-Bipartisan-Failure

economic theory, however ingenious, will also not create a new type of man (and woman) and will not recreate the family and marriage, which is the necessary engine behind any functioning economy. No one was more concerned with the human rot at the center of our cities than Jack Kemp, and like Moynihan the destruction of the family and marriage. One does not live by bread alone, and however necessary bread is, what it takes to create the bakery in the first place is a great deal of human capital. And, the great Achilles heel of capitalism is its powerlessness to reproduce and recreate men, the very kind of men and women required to make an economy fruitful and productive.[155] All the economic freedom and opportunity in the world is no good if there is not the capacity to responsibly exercise the dominion that God has gifted humanity with from the outset (Genesis 1:28-30, 9:1-3). For cities to "push back" against the prevailing Tower of Babel that the nation state is becoming, requires a renewed and regenerated humanity. We need a vision that both undergirds and transcends economic theory. Hence, we need an entirely new type, symbol and theological construct.

The new type or symbol of the city is what points the way forward, and this is a woman, the bride at the end of the Bible. The very image, the very type that gives us an entire mindset is the Bride of Christ, the New Jerusalem.

---

155 The older world of apprenticeship was able to do this. Our social atomization is pulverizing this capacity, and it must be found anew, somehow, someway. A fatherless world that idolizes youth, instead of a world where youth emulate older models, becomes its own conundrum and contradiction.

STARTING OVER WITH THE CITY

In our previous chapter, we reached the very beginning of the Bible, and this is where Rosenstock-Huessy's excavation of the great revolutions ends. He published his great book in 1938, and it is now and nearly 80 years beyond that date. We must once again be revolutionary. We must go back to the end of the Bible once more. We are now beginning to cycle through the Bible once more. One great cycle has been completed. There is only one pericope beyond the Last Judgment where Rosenstock-Huessy began and that is the New Jerusalem. The final city is the new model of what must be. It is a city that has walls, but is not protected by them. There are boundaries, but the gates are opened all the time, and there is no temple in the midst of the city. There is no cathedral, because the entire city is now, as a perfect cube, the Holy of Holies. City and temple have merged into one. This of course, is the final vision in the Eschaton. Here, there still is not finality and perfection. Here we still have the divisions of Church and state, and the obvious reality of individual marriages. But the final image provides a telos, an end, that provides orientation in the here and now, in the same way that the Fatherhood of God in the here and now, provides a model, a type, an image of earthly fatherhood, which will be completely fulfilled in the eternal state.

After the fall of the Roman Empire, there was a passion for the rebuilding of cities, because cities had been lost with the collapse of civilization. The model for the rebuilding of cities was the Classical world. The models were Rome, Athens and the theory of the Greek City State. Indeed, modern nation states owe something to the Greek ideal of the city state.

The model is no longer the Classical world. The model is the New Jerusalem. The city is the ganglion, and the meeting place of the new tribes and empire of the global economy. This new city is not a Greek City State, but a model of the city where God meets with and lives in fellowship with His people. Can we now start over again with the New Jerusalem?

THE NEW JERUSALEM AND THE MEANING OF POSTMODERNITY

Jesus came as the New Emperor of the world. He came as the King of kings. His enthronement actually began with His crucifixion, with the Cross being His first throne. As a king, He died for His people, but He was raised up and ascended into Heaven to be seated at the right hand of the Father.

As the new Emperor, He is the master of both space and time. With the conquest of each territory has come a new historical consciousness. In a not yet conscious way, the human race has been reviving one form of consciousness after another for the last two thousand years. We have now reached the place where some form of consciousness from every time period of history has to some degree been rehabilitated by the Church somewhere on the earth. Each revolution has rehabilitated some aspect of man that was first created in the era before Christ. We have now reached the point of becoming conscious of this recreation, and we mistake its meaning.[156] Apart from Christ Himself, who has been the rehabilitator, we have now become conscious of what has been happening, and we mistake it for relativistic historical consciousness. One might term it post-modernity, and we mistake it for a radical relativization, but it is no such thing. Rather, we have now reached the place of the City, The New Jerusalem, where some from every people, tribe, tongue and nation, will be or where some from every range of historical consciousness will be. This is where the paradox of Revelation 21:26-27 will find its fulfillment: "And they shall bring the glory and honor of the nations into it. But there shall by no means enter it anything that defiles, or causes an abomination...." For the Jew, the nations by definition were unclean, and yet that is who is entering here, which is the Most Holy Place.[157]   Every historical

---

156 134 Lectures 1-25. Rosenstock-Huessy, E. (1992). Universal History-1954. H. R. Huessy, Hans R. Huessy.

"...the first era covers perhaps the years from 10,000 BC to 3000 BC, the era of the empires covers the time of 3000 BC to 1911 of our era, as I tried to tell--show you. In the years between 1911 and 1918, five empires were destroyed: China, India, Germany, Russia, Austria-Hungary. So the last empires went, you see. There is no emperor of India anymore. There is no emperor of Austria. There is no emperor of Germany. There is no emperor of Russia. There is no emperor in China. That's quite a story...You never hear that in history that the world wars really were fought to force the last remnants of pre-Christian orders, you see, into the common history of the human race. That's why the empires, the different worlds, had to go." (3-17) February 18, 1954

157 The New Jerusalem is a perfect cube (twelve thousand furlongs in length, breadth, and height) which, though it is a symbolic number, if taken literally would be about fourteen hundred miles cubed, and would be about the size of the entirety of the United States east of the Mississippi. The reason it is a perfect cube is because the Holy of Holies in both the Tabernacle and Temple was a perfect cube. The entire city is a Holy of Holies where all of God's people live in perfect fellowship and presence of God as his priestly nation. The entrance of anything unclean into the Holy of Holies rises above the level of mere uncleanness to "abomination".

consciousness now is cleansed when it bows before Jesus Christ.

One of my subheadings is "Global Empire and Tribalism as Anodynes to One Another." This follows a section in which it becomes clear that the three forms of human configuration, the tribal, the monarchical and empire, have all been passed through once in Western history. We have also completed one cycle of Hope, Love and Faith, as the lead theological virtues. Coming to the time of the New Jerusalem is the new configuration that moves beyond what has transpired before.

How does this fit with the fact that Augustine (354-430 AD) wrote *The City of God* sometime before the 21st century? It is a seminal work, and the first book of Biblical theology. Are we only now beginning to catch up to Augustine? In many ways, yes. Augustine's *City of God* says very little about actual cities. "City" for Augustine is a metaphor for the two kinds of humanity, the regenerate and the unregenerate. Now the metaphor is merging with the literal and the factual and points to humanity's global metropolizing as well.

THE NEW JERUSALEM, THE NEW UNIVERSITY, AND RENEWED CIVILIZATION

This final place is the vision of the New Jerusalem. This will ground the university and civilization for the next five hundred years or whatever period of time is required for us to absorb and digest the new availability of all forms of human consciousness. The city is the mingling place of all

---

This raises the level of oxymoron in the passage to the greatest level.

forms of consciousness, and the university, par excellence, is the place of comparison and contrast of all mindsets. But difference of mind cannot be tolerated apart from unity of heart. Unity of heart can only be found with the outworking of a consciousness of every tribe, tongue, nation and people being a part of this new polis, this new Christendom, the New Jerusalem.

The Bible ends with two cosmic cities in the book of Revelation (chapters 17-22). The New Jerusalem, which represents the New Heaven and the New Earth, is the outcome of the New Covenant in Jesus Christ. At the very end of the Bible, it comes down from Heaven and appears to hover over the earth and is very near. The book of Hebrews assures us that we have now come to the city of the living God, the New Jerusalem (Hebrews 12:22). It is a present as well as future reality. It is something like corporate headquarters of the Kingdom of God.[158]

Likewise, Babylon the Great is also an on-going present reality, and it represents all of fallen humanity's attempts to find sufficiency and life apart from God. For a time, it is a very rich, and in many ways, successful city. It is a city of merchandise, and the merchandise indicates the economic conquests of that city. It has merchandise of "gold, silver, precious stones and pearls, fine linen and purple, silk and scarlet, every kind of citron wood, every kind of object of most precious wood, bronze, iron, and marble...." and much more (Rev. 18:12). But it is also a city of corruption, decadence and violence. Ultimately, the mark of its commerce is that it trades in the "bodies and souls of men."

---

158 https://m.facebook.com/story.php?story_fbid=815124448524086&id=137855609584310&_rdr

(vs. 13). It is the "dwelling place of demons, a prison for every foul spirit and a cage for every unclean and hated bird...." (Rev. 18:2). It is finally a city that is "drunk with blood."

These images are especially relevant for us because we are living in a time when the entire planet is metropolizing. Everywhere human beings are leaving their rural roots and are moving into the city. In China every year, thirty million people are leaving farms and rural life and are moving into cities. That, as one of my professors reminded us, is the entire population of Canada moving annually into the city in that great nation. This phenomena is global on every continent and in virtually every nation. So it behooves us to study the city and to find a theology of the city.

TYPOLOGY, HISTORY AND SOCIOLOGY OF THE NEW JERUSALEM, AND BABYLON THE GREAT

It is also true that typology and symbolism cut to the truth faster and with more clarity than a hundred sophisticated sociological studies ever could, and the Biblical images cut to the chase almost instantly on this theme.

Most languages have masculine and feminine nouns, and I am not sure these are entirely arbitrary. The gender of nouns may convey very deep truths that need to be unearthed. The "city" is in the feminine gender in most languages. Both of the cities at the Bible's end are feminine, and both are symbolized by women.

Biblical imagery is fluid and traverses the depths of

meaning by what it immediately transforms into. If one looks the first time, one sees a city. But, if one blinks, what is seen with the second look is not a city, but a woman. In both cases they are beautiful women, and both are possessed of glory. But one is corrupt and is the woman of death, and the second is faithful and true and is filled with infinite life. The first city is Babylon the Great who becomes the Whore of Babylon. The second is the New Jerusalem who becomes the Bride of Christ.

Now here we find an intertwining of two things that in some mystical and final sense belong together. It is also the fascinating case that, empirically in the modern world, they belong together. The power of sexual relationship and the fact of a metropolis belong together. The city is the great trysting place, the place of renewal or destruction of relationship, the place where souls and bodies are bought and sold, or where truth and fidelity create new life. They do so in the text, and they do so in reality.

This point is critical to the orientation of the advisor to the king. First, because it offers an explanation and understanding that most, if not all leaders, civic and academic, must come to grips with. The crisis underlying the chaos is played out sexually and symbolically in the areas the leader has governance over. And, secondly, the contest between the New Jerusalem and Babylon over the symbol of marriage, masculinity and femininity offers a prescriptive solution for the leader.

THE EROTIC AND THE CITY

Socrates was very willing to pay the price exacted upon him by his city because he owed his existence and being to it. And the "it" was not an "it" but a "she" and "she" was a mother to him. Our respective cities ought to function as mothers giving us life, and nourishing and protecting us after our birth. But our cities are not without either husband or master, and all belong to God, or gods who father through them and lend their character and name. In the ancient world, every city had some titular god or gods to whom she was beholden. Prostitution was, more often than not, sacred prostitution. The prostitute was a gateway to the god whom he or she served. To have intercourse with a sacred prostitute was to consort with the gods, and this sexualized relationship defined the underlying energy of the city. The temple was the center of the city, and the center of the temple was the sexual commerce of the temple.

The ancient world was, with qualified exceptions (exceptions that gave rise to both expansive and cultural energy), overwhelmingly given to polymorphous sexuality. The issue was not one of gender. That is, the issue was not one of male and female, but one of penetrator and penetratee, and it did not much matter what was penetrated by the aggressive party. It might be boys, girls, men, women or animals. And while romantic love did exist within marriage (as the story of Helen of Troy, or Penelope and Odysseus remind us) it was a rare aristocratic luxury and did not in principle exclude other forms of sexual expression, especially for the man. And when chastity was imposed, it was universally imposed on the woman and not on the man.

The sexualization and exclusiveness of marriage was the gift of the Torah.[159] The Torah restricted sexual intercourse to the heterosexual union that was bound in covenant, and in the Law of the Old Testament we see the gradual move away from polygamy to a monogamous standard. The model for both parenting and for marriage as found in the Old Testament is found in Yahweh's relationship as Father to Israel and Jerusalem and finally as Husband. All peoples model themselves on their gods, and Israel likewise modeled herself on the God she belonged to.

Further, the Bible is the real source of the freeing of women. As far back as Genesis 2:24, ("Therefore shall a man shall leave his father and his mother, and shall cleave unto his wife; and they shall be one flesh.") there is opposition to the clan structure, which is the real source of female oppression.[160] This is worthy of an entire paper, and I can only touch on it here. But briefly, in the clan system (which is ubiquitous outside of the world shaped by the Old and New Testaments and is utterly dominant in all of Islam), the young new bride counts for nothing when the son brings his new wife home to live in his parent's home. It is the matriarch, the mother, who has final say and authority. If there is disagreement between the mother and the bride (and this is one of the primary rivalries within the clan structure), the son will always side with his mother over against his bride.[161] This is, in fact, much the source

---

159 http://catholiceducation.org/articles/homosexuality/ho0003.html

160 See especially, Rosenstock-Huessy's *Out of Revolution*, Chapter 13, "The Survival of Austria-Hungary, and pages 616-617.

161 In the clan system, the eldest son is more often than not, the real protector and defender of the mother, and not her husband.

of ubiquitous wife beating that always transpires within the clan system.[162] He beats his wife to please his mother, who was likewise treated as a young bride. When the son is enjoined to leave his father and mother and cleave to his wife (and this is the source of the nuclear family as opposed to the clan), she becomes the most important and influential person in his life. Historical development begins to be sped up because of this differentiation, and what she brings from her father's household that is different. In the clan system she can bring almost nothing (she is expected to become part of the landscape, and anything different would be regarded a threat), and little or nothing changes or develops. Genesis 2:24 creates a new kind of world in which the woman is the dramatic source of social and societal development.

But the even more radical difference made by the Torah in relationship to marriage had to do with the underlying metaphysics. In the Roman Empire, for example, there were hundreds of cults and religions. They all, however, had underlying characteristics that were similar. All of them were dependent on an underlying monism or pantheism. This was not always the bald monism that became the defining characteristic of the Vedas or of what we would now describe as Eastern religion but underneath the differentiation of being that existed at the surface level, at a much deeper level, there was a shared unity and power. Sexual energy was one of the shared powers or energies

---

162 Americans and Europeans are shocked by wife beating, even though it can transpire with frequency, especially as marriage and family bonds decay, but are almost never aware of how much it is simply part of the accepted landscape of any and all parts of the world that have never been Christianized.

that defined the unity and also the divinity of being. The religious, monistic and divine nature of sexual energy is most explicit in a text like *The Kama Sutra*[163] and in the discipline of tantric sex but it is implicit in all of paganism. To penetrate would be the sign of power and dominion, but to be penetrated meant to overwhelm, engulf and swallow the other in a great ocean of being. In all of this, there was participation in the underlying divinity of the cosmos.

The one religion in the ancient world that denied the identity of sexual energy with divinity was Judaism. The Torah, alone in the ancient world, confined sexual expression to marriage and denied the polymorphous sexualization of all being. Christianity followed Judaism and carried the theme of complete fidelity within monogamous marriage forward in the great image of Christ and His Bride as the Church. That now began to redefine the city. The city was not to be an expression of ancient polymorphous sexuality, but an expression of the one and only bond, of God's unique and faithful relationship in monogamy with His Bride. Hence, something relatively new appeared on the scene. There were precursors to this in the inter-testamental period with the Jews while they were still under the rule of Persia, Greece and Rome, but those precursors were now greatly magnified and expanded. From that point on, the ancient city, which rested upon the foundations of sexualized monism, was to be challenged by another city which was defined by Christ's faithful marriage. The challenge was complete and total. Both visions of the city and sex

---

163 V*atsy*ayana, M. R. Anand, et al. (1982). *Kama Sutra*. New Delhi Atlantic Highlands, N.J., Published by Sanskrit Pratishthan for Arnold-Heinemann; Humanities Press.

cannot be the foundation of the world. One or the other will ultimately predominate. From that point on, pagan polymorphous sexualized monism was to be challenged by Christian monogamy. Hence, just as a wounded animal will lash back with fatal defensiveness, now, polymorphous sexuality will also lash back at its challenger. It has always been defined by domination and submission, but as with everything else in the ancient world (all of the principalities and powers) it was far more benign in the ancient world than now. In the ancient world, apart from the challenge of Israel (which was comparatively small and localized), the polymorphous sexuality threatened to become universal and to completely displace what was previously normative. For a time Christianity pushed it back into the shadows, but since the Renaissance polymorphous sexuality began expanding anew so that now it has taken on the character of anti-Christ. What was implicit but often hidden is now explicit and radicalized. Polymorphous sexuality would now evolve to become sado-masochistic, violent and blood thirsty (as became evident in the in the games and colosseum of the late collapsing Roman Empire). Hence domination and submission are radicalized and become one of the means of seeking a perverse salvation. It ultimately becomes the worship of death. We see in a figure like the Marquis de Sade torture and murder become means of achieving orgasm and satisfaction. Modern serial murder is almost always tied to pulsating orgasmic pleasure, and pornography, as it descends from softcore to hardcore, is defined by how much it relies upon inflicting and receiving pain.

Hence, the beast, the kings and the woman are all now

ultimately defined by what they hate. The woman is "drunk with the blood of the saints," the beast is "filled with names of blasphemy" and the kings "make war with the Lamb." They are all defined as against the Kingdom of God that has now been established and in competition with them. The sexual relations of the woman, the kings and the beast are entirely made up of what we would now term sado-masochism. The kings that she gives herself to are themselves beholden to a power superior to them, and this power is termed the beast. The woman also has direct relations with the beast, and the biblical language and imagery indicate bestiality. She has intercourse not only with the kings, but also the beast upon whom she is seated. It is lust fueled by pain, domination, slavish submission, hatred and rebellion. The danger of any woman giving herself to more than one man is that the men involved will either not value her, or, if they do, they will be afflicted with great jealousy. These relationships eventually become violent and destructive. The text finally tells us that the ten kings in the end "hate the harlot, make her desolate and naked, eat her flesh and burn her with fire," (Revelation 17:16).

Both of these cities are now active historical powers. Both are now at work and active on the human scene. Real cities in the real world partake of the reality of both of these cities right now. No city in the world is entirely one city or the other. But for every city, especially now as the Gospel is taken to all of the world, both of these realities are at work.

While these are symbolic types, what is clear from the Bible is that the Gnostic dualism between symbol and fact does not exist. The question is never a choice between whether something belongs to the realm of fact or to the realm of symbol and value. There is no dualism of this sort. The symbolism of the two women and the kind of covenants (or anti-covenants) that they live in extends to the real sexual and marital relationships that real men and women live in, in the real cities of the world. A city that worships like Babylon the Great will be a city that models its sexual relationships after the harlot, the beast and the kings. A city that worships as a part of the New Jerusalem will model its marital covenants after the Bride and her Husband.

The question is which city will dominate in any given city in the world in which we live. One city is corrupt and lives ultimately by trading in "the souls of men...." (Rev 17:13) and is under judgment. It is a city given to destruction. The other city is the city of the glory of God and the glorified humanity. It is the place where ultimately all human potentialities are fulfilled, and it is finally blessed with no curse. What is most important for our purposes in this paper is that the first city is marked by sexual debauchery and what could be termed relations that are sado-masochistic. The second is marked by fidelity and love in the bonds of marriage.

Biblically, there are two great erotic forces at work in history. They are the New Jerusalem, the Bride of Christ, and Babylon the Great, the Whore of Babylon. The second case (of which all of us by nature partake) is at heart sado/masochistic. She nourishes herself with human blood, and her lovers eventually hate her, devour her flesh and give her over to be burned with fire (Revelation 17:17). This is a picture of all destructive eroticism at work in history and a picture of just what we need sanctified out of us. The picture of the New Jerusalem, the Bride of Christ, is the opposite .

The power of the erotic is hardly taken into account at all in the modern church. However badly worked out, at least the medieval church understood the reality. The great ancient teacher of the power of the erotic was Plato. The great modern non-Christian teacher and one of the most influential and powerful formers of the modern world was Rousseau. We tend to think of Kant as forming his great project in reaction to Hume's critique of causality (and that is true), but primarily Kant (who was the unsexiest of men) formed his project as a theoretical underpinning of Rousseau's erotic vision. He wanted eventually to make a place for the sublime. The great flowering of German culture in the 19th century was eventually a stream that had its headwaters in Rousseau.[164]

America is Rousseau gone rotten. Feeling, sentiment and compassion all stripped of any profundity are most of the underpinning for most of current liberal ethos. The easy availability of sexual intercourse on American campuses, and in American urban life, is lobotomizing us and destroying most capacity for any hunger for spiritual reality. If there is any hunger, it is connected to the vagueness of Eastern mysticism, which is easily compatible with an animal hunger for orgasm. Since we have forgotten The Song of Solomon, we have been overtaken by Hugh Hefner and all of his cheap imitators. Fine wines are unnecessary as long as one has enough of cheap distilled liquors that might blind one and certainly numb all the sensibilities.

Almost without exception, our apologetics are consumed with the rational/scientific side of things, but the

---

164 Allan Bloom, (1993) *Love & Friendship* New York, Simon and Schuster. 72, 83

existential realities of most young people are flat eroticism, and to this we have almost nothing to say except that as Christians we believe in chastity. I am convinced that if we are to make any headway we have to learn what erotic imagination is and how to speak to it. It is a huge theme in the Bible. It is at least as big as it is in Plato and Rousseau. We had better recover what is really there. And the heart of what is really there can be gotten at very quickly in this final pericope of Scripture: the New Jerusalem as juxtaposed against Babylon the Great. Both of these great pictures embody the erotic as a fundamental force of either fidelity and truth in marriage and the Great Marriage or of promiscuity, destruction and sado-masochism. These images intersect perfectly with the reality of the city, which is inescapably going to be our environment as we move ever closer to the consummation of history. Hence, the handle that can be grasped in moving toward renewal of both city and university is marriage, Christian marriage. Here the micro and the macro merge and become one.

MARRIAGE AND THE CITY

All of this would imply that whoredom is the great overlap with the tohu and bohu, the chaos of Genesis 1:2. Whoredom is essentially a complete metaphor for moral and spiritual chaos. The great life work of the French Calvinist scholar, Denis DeRougemont, may be finding its culmination in our own time.[165] A simple summary of his thesis is that Western Civilization has, since the twelfth

---

165 Rougemont, D. d. and M. Beigion (1940). *Love in the western world*. New York, Harcourt.

century, struggled with the suppression, and consequent repression, of the ideal of passionate love. We have forgotten that the origin of the meaning of passion is to suffer. The idea that appears to have had its origins in the Albigensian heresy, that love is beautiful "to the extent that it is woeful," appears to have been a reaction to the Christian doctrine of marriage. "At all times and in all places the natural growth of what I call passionate love has been visible. Alike in Greece and Rome and in the East the frenzy of passion was treated as simply a frenzy and nothing more. Not until the twelfth century, the century of Abélard, Saint Bernard, the Troubadours and Tristan-and then in Western Europe, did the natural seeds of passion, instead of being destroyed, suddenly begin to be cultivated. The love frenzy was raised to the level of a religious wisdom. It was given symbolic expression that made it acceptable, a dignified form, and a rhetoric that endowed it with standing. Unfortunate love was admitted to be beautiful and good to the extent it was woeful."[166] Adultery and all of its glorious miseries became the predominate theme of literature from that time until its apparent destruction in various times and places in the twentieth century. Beginning with the Tristan myth, which has reincarnated itself in almost an infinite variety of ways (from King Arthur's Camelot, to Tolstoy's Anna Karenina, through Flaubert's Madam Bovary and Theodore Driser's Sister Carrie, to every cheap romantic novel and soap opera), the theme of forbidden love and adultery as opposed to happy marriage (which has been portrayed as hopelessly boring and enslaving) has dominated the Western imagination. That time appears to be over. It is so

---

166 Ibid. P. v

much over that it prompted Allan Bloom to complain that the primary disaster prompted by feminism has been the destruction of the Western canon of literature.[167] Feminism has destroyed the predominance of the Tristan myth, and all of the consequent pleasures of the agonies of adultery, because it has completely undermined Christian marriage, which the myth must be a parasite upon. We have now descended to pure whoredom.

DeRougemont made similar observations about Europe and Russia in her revolutionary melt down period between the great World Wars. Both Stalin and Hitler later found it necessary to reincarnate marriage and family bonds for purely utilitarian and statist reasons.[168] This followed periods of complete sexual lassitude, the forbidding of marriage, the encouragement of abortion and the abandonment of infants. Both post revolutionary Russia, and, famously, the Weimar Republic descended to almost complete sexual and moral chaos.[169] Anyone acquainted with campus and dormitory life on American campuses today know that it is not very different.[170] When one surveys the current European landscape, one sees particularly the famously liberated Dutch Republic, which is appallingly close in ambiance to the Weimar Republic. One wonders if the final outcome will not be similar to the outcome imposed by the great dictators of the Thirties. We

167 Bloom, A. D. (1987). *The closing of the American mind.* New York, Simon and Schuster.   pp. 97-108

168 Rougemont, D. d. and M. Beigion (1940). *Love in the Western World.* New York,, Harcourt. pp. 272-278

169 Ibid. pp.259-278

170 Wolfe, T. (2004). *I am Charlotte Simmons.* New York, Farrar, Straus, Giroux.

are back to the dialectic of chaos and complete control.[171]

This is not the first venture with such outcomes. The collapse of Rome was famously so, and one remembers that in the aftermath of the French Revolution the mob at one point enthroned a harlot and named her Reason. It seems the inevitable outcome to worshipping the chaos.[172]

The theory would tell us that the answer is also to be found in this last pericope of Scripture: the great resurgence of Christian marriage as both a literal reality, and the type of the new city is the key and the new handle to Jesus bringing renewal. The leaders of both university and city need this great immediate image and reality as a way of finding the way forward. For upward of eight centuries, perhaps culminating literarily in Flaubert's *Madam Bovary*, and sociologically in Betty Friedan's *The Feminine Mystique*, marriage is finally suffocated by the great bourgeois haters.[173] Marriage had successfully been defined by its

---

171 The illegitimacy rate in the United States is now 40%. A civilized order cannot sustain this, and it points to a future of very complete statist control. http://gunnyg.wordpress.com/2009/03/01/ann-coulter-wrong-on-illegitimacy-rates-by-david-r-usher/

172 "Sometimes a man has been heard to declare that he wishes both to enjoy the advantage of high culture and to abolish compulsory continence. The inherent desire of the human organism, however, seems to be such that these desires are incompatible, or even contradictory. Any human society is free to choose either to display great energy or to enjoy sexual freedom: the evidence is that it cannot do both for more than one generation." Unwin, J. D. (1934). *Sex and Culture*. London, Oxford University Press, H. Milford. p. 412

173 *The Feminine Mystique,* published 19 February 1963 is a book written by Betty Friedan, published by W.W. Norton and company which brought to light the lack of fulfillment in many women's lives, which was generally kept hidden. According to *The New York Times* obituary of Friedan in 2006, it "ignited the contemporary women's movement in 1963 and as a result permanently transformed the social fabric of the United States and countries around the world" and "is widely regarded as one of the most influential nonfiction books of the 20th century."

enemies (the descendants of the Albigensians) so that it finally became an easy kill. It is perhaps only now that true Christian marriage can become the great new symbol and type of the next new Christian era, the era of the city.

We are about to enter a new era of world history. How will it come? The last time it came, it came by means of God conquering the impossible and overcoming barriers that were superhuman. That is how God does it every time He does a new thing. The last time, He overcame the remnants of the old paganism that were still resident in the Western mind and soul. If anyone goes to India and observes the still regnant idols that many of the people are in thralldom to, it will be seen that these idols are really horrible, bloodthirsty, murderous, devouring, demons. They hate humanity and long to enslave and even destroy it. In the West, God had through a thousand years taught the human race that it was sinful and that at the same time He was just. Beyond that, the Christian Gospel also taught that God, in His mercy was redeeming humanity, and herein was the tension. When the explosion of the Reformation came, this tension culminated. The Reformation came to Europe by enabling them to take hold on something that was seemingly impossible and had

---

The Feminine Mystique came about after Friedan sent a questionnaire to other women in her 1942 Smith College graduating class. Most women in her class indicated a general unease with their lives. Through her findings, Friedan hypothesized that women are victims of a false belief system that requires them to find identity and meaning in their lives through their husbands and children. Such a system causes women to completely lose their identity in that of their family.

Friedan specifically locates this system among post-World War II middle-class suburban communities. She suggests that men returning from war turned to their wives for mothering. At the same time, America's post-war economic boom had led to the development of new technologies that were supposed to make household work less difficult, but that often had the result of making women's work less meaningful and valuable.

http://en.wikipedia.org/wiki/The_Feminine_Mystique

been a growing tension for 500 years: that God was not a blood thirsty god, and He did not want to trap the race and destroy it, using its own sinfulness against it, but was a God who was so great that He could forgive human beings and overcome His own righteous anger by means of mercy. God could overcome God, and mercy could triumph over wrath and justice. This was impossible, utterly impossible. In Europe, men still were close enough to the old empire and tribal paganisms to feel what humanity in India still feel. By faith, one could find mercy in a just God. It is hard for us to relate to the quandary that the human race felt in those days.

The Reformation came through Justification by Faith. The new era will come through a new emblem: marriage. It is the image of marriage as combined with the image of the city in the picture of the New Jerusalem in Revelation 21-22. Marriage is the new emblem and type of the new configuration of the human race. The two are combined in Revelation 21-22, but marriage is impossible. Ask almost anyone under thirty, and, if they won't say it, they feel it. It is impossible. That is why such a high percentage of them are living together without benefit of marriage. They have watched their parents and seen too much for too long. The experience is too deep and they are too knowledgeable. The thing is impossible. One had just as well not even try. Just hook up and have a roommate with privileges for a while. And even more fearful is the thought of having a family. Lots of girls want a baby, but the only thing that is more fearful to young men than marriage is the thought of being a father. That is the horror of horrors. And on top of that, we are now facing the fears of worldwide depression.

Who in their right mind would take on the most extended financial obligation of all in a world like ours? Marriage is impossible.

There is only one way to be married. One must be married by faith. It is as impossible in our time as believing in forgiveness was in Luther's time. And the only alternative to the image of marriage as we find it in Revelation 21 and 22, as we metropolize all over the world, is the image of whoredom in Revelation 18. This tells the whole story of the hell that humanity is doomed to in the city if we do not marry successfully. The Whore of Babylon who drinks blood and is herself destroyed by her pimps is the other possible picture as the alternative to the picture of the New Jerusalem. This is also a picture of economic devastation. The whore and her pimps not only devour blood, but every form of wealth. It is all squandered in the most horrible of orgies. Sex and death are very expensive, and generations of capital can be devoured in one night of revelry. Whoever is right about the technical source of our vast mal-investment, at heart it is whoredom that undoes everything. Marriage is impossible. The city is also impossible. The university is impossible. But these need not be impossible, either on the micro or the macro level. But it happens in only one way: by faith. And marriage is the type that is at the heart of each of these realities. And the reality of all of these types is the Church, the Bride of Christ. Marriage by faith is where the new world is going to come from. It is impossible in every other way.[174]

---

174 It is true that one of the revolutions inspired by Luther was the re-introduction of clerical marriage, and his marriage to Katy was one of the most important relationships in the history and development of the Western Christian world. Never-the-less, for Luther, marriage was

It was recently suggested to me that young professionals and graduate students have descended to the level of Roman slaves.[175] Slaves were allowed to have sexual liaisons, but were not usually permitted to marry. They were not permitted to marry, because they could be sold on the market at any moment their masters so determined. Likewise, modern young professionals and graduate students often do not marry after co-habitating for years, because they know that the forces of the market can call them away from one another at any moment. Hence, liaisons, but not marriages, are made.

It is marriage that will give to the market its proper boundaries and structure. Markets are good, and, apart from markets, real freedom or economic viability is inconceivable. But the market cannot be sovereign over all of human activity. It is the very mark of Babylon the Great that it trades in the "bodies and souls of men…." (Revelation 18:13). Marriage by faith will tell markets that they cannot transgress the boundaries of that relationship and what is closest to it.

Every era needs an image, an idea, a pericope of Scripture to live by. This has historically been given by God as we are called into a new world. The City and the Bride I believe, are that pericope. This is the image that leaders in the new city must themselves be captured by and live by as they call those around and under them to newness and hope in the creation of a new world.

a consequence and outgrowth of the Reformation, not the cause of it. Marriage is now moving to being the causal and central reality of the new world that God is creating.

175 This was suggested by Peter Escalante in a phone conversation on Saturday, March 14, 2009

Afterword

WHERE THE RUBBER MEETS THE ROAD

"Welcome to our town...." I have welcomed a number of officials to our town. After one of our luncheons in which the pastors had invited a university official to speak about his work, I can still remember sitting at my desk in my office the next day and very self consciously thinking to myself, "I can pick up the telephone, and invite this gentleman to have lunch with me...or not." It was one of those luminous moments that changed my life, but at the time it seemed utterly pedestrian and ordinary. It is only in retrospect that I can see the momentousness that I faced at my desk.

I picked up the telephone, and I dialed this official. My first surprise was how easy he was to reach. I explained who I was in connection to our lunch the day before. He accepted my invitation. That was my second surprise. I began for the first time to understand the authority and voice that I had with public officials as a pastor who represented, not my denomination, but the Kingdom of God along with the other pastors in our city. We met for lunch, and my next surprise was how anxious he was to talk with me, and it was clear that he was not a particularly religious person, but he was happy to have someone to whom he could unburden himself. He apparently did not feel he had to impress me or speak with me as any kind of partisan. This official met with me several times and to a remarkable degree opened his heart. He was a tough, somewhat hard-boiled, no nonsense official who was brought in specifically to get things done because the person at the top was proving to not be so capable, but was still politically untouchable. It was quite a lesson.

Over the years, some of these relationships blossomed into more than I could have imagined at that point. In those years, I began to learn to knit together what I wrote about early in this Manifesto in regard to what Doctor Tournier made so explicit concerning the repression of the Kingdom of God with the realities that Rosenstock-Huessy unveiled for us in the great revolutions of the Christian West. One must deal with both the repressed and the trajectory. One must both speak the unspeakable (the repressed) and also present the aim. These are not so far apart since purpose is also part of the repressed in our era of scienticism and reductionism.[176] To finally begin to be able to lead leaders to the knowledge that the city and the renewal of marriage are the place we are going is to at least give them hope and sometimes some sense of what steps to begin to take to move toward.

---

176 This simple but profound point has been at the very center of the work of both the great philosopher of science, Michael Polanyi, and the great American Reformed philosopher, Alvin Plantinga.

HOPE, JUDGMENT AND THE PROPHETIC

We are at the end of an era. I do not believe my country is going to be renewed to be what it once was any more than Israel, after falling into idolatry and decay, ever again achieved the greatness and splendor of the monarchs of David and Solomon. In the end, God does something new. The era of the nation state that replaced the medieval configuration of Christendom is nearing its end. The glories of our Declaration of Independence, Constitution and the Founding Fathers are not going to come back however sympathetic I may be with many of the sentiments and hopes of those who are assiduously working toward this. God brings judgment, and He brings things to an end. He also brings resurrection and renewal, but He does it in a new way. As pastors, we are called to be prophetic.

It is hard to know how things gel in the spirit, but here is what happened to me at one point several years ago. Slowly, morning by morning, the Titanic began changing course. At a certain point, I began to have a conviction, and a "word" came to me (if I may sound so charismatic). It began to come to me that part of my calling was to simply go about and announce that judgment had come. That is all. I was not to explain, I was not to embellish, at least very much. If people ask me how I think that is so, or what I meant, I was not to explain, but rather get very Rogerian[177] and ask them what they think it means.

---

177 Carl Rogers (1902-1987), the founder of "Person Centered Therapy" which emphasized "empathy" and "reflecting back" to clients their feelings and thoughts. I am not endorsing Rogerianism here as a full scale therapy option, I am simply using it as a descriptor. http://carlrogers.info/

I began to do this. I found that people already knew this is true, but had not thought of it in any theological term. People's consciousness had already been breached. It is always better for people to explain to themselves what they know than explain it for them (David says to Nathan, "That man shall die...." and it is much more powerful than Nathan saying, "You deserve to die....")

The results have been interesting, to say the least. It sets people thinking in ways they have never thought before.

Here is an e-mail post I wrote to some friends several years ago:

"I told you a week or so ago that I felt called to go about and announce judgment. I thought you might be interested in how it is going. Well, I have since preached once, been invited to teach an adult Sunday School class at a Baptist church, and met with several pastors. And, I have talked with a bunch of people. Yesterday, I had an appointment for the first time with_____ and tomorrow, I meet with_____ The feeling I am having now is a little bit like some mental play acting that N.T. Wright does when he imagines Paul leaving one more city he has gone to, and saying to himself in reference to preaching the Cross and the Resurrection, "I can't believe it: it worked again."

"I am sure that I will begin to hit some hard cases who either will not hear or will be angry, but not yet. So far, I am rather amazed."

"Yesterday, I met wih _____. Before going in to see him, I telephoned a friend and asked him to pray for me. He asked me if I was going to lay my "judgment thing" on him. I said I did not know; I always play these things by ear to feel my way forward and see how it seems. But, indeed,

I did. I laid it on thick. His response was, "Nobody talks about these things...you must come back soon and we will talk some more." Now, you must know, I did not walk in on a pagan. He is a serious Roman Catholic, and he even works with the local Caring Pregnancy Center, so he is perhaps not a "hard case" in the first place. But _____ had the sense I had (and I want to generalize a bit here) that indeed all of these people in positions like his know something of the truth. Their budgetary concerns are enormous. They do not just know we are broke theoretically; they are living with it day in and day out. They are, under it all, sick of smoke and mirrors, happy faces, pretend optimism. The odd thing is that when you say, "we are under judgment." it feels real to them, and oddly it gives them hope. Yes, judgment gives birth to hope. It means there is meaning to this and we can respond to a Personal Agent. My old friend, the_____ used to say over and over after his reconversion, "I just want to learn whatever it is that I am suppose to so we can get on from this...." Openness. That is the key. That is what I was able to communicate to him. "What must we do?" is the question. Well, I don't know what someone in his position does who is the leader of the one of the very influential institutions in our world. But I can say, "Well, the point is to ask, and keep asking, 'What do we do?' "

I have been reading the prophets a lot. They are hard to read. There is not very much "story" in them, and indeed, the stereotype of them is not untrue. It is mostly a lot of denunciation, fulmination, pronouncement of doom. But put in the larger context, it makes sense. The underlying problems were, pride, idolatry, and then the consequent oppression. Over and over, in place after place (the Egyptians, Babylonians, Persians, and above all, Israel and Judah). It is a monotonous message, because we are so thick. So Israel got "cured" in the Babylonian Captivity and immediately took up to transform old fashioned childish idolatry into the high powered beginnings of humanism that are still with us. Just as every covenant has a "Gentile Sponsor" so it is with the Jews after Babylon. The Greeks become the "Gentile Sponsor" of the new false covenant, and together the Jews and the Greeks develop humanism. That, I believe, is much of the meaning of the "intra-Testamental period" and of course is the new battle that Jesus has when He arrives. The Judaizers are those who want to push all of the world into this hybrid form of humanism to infect the Church, which has definitively broken this mold. Then the Church with the collapse of the Classical world moves out to convert the tribes (old fashioned childish idolatry) and by the time of the Reformation and Renaissance, begins its modern battle with advanced idolatry, which is still with us. The university is at the heart of this humanism. God is now speaking to this in our post 9/11 world.

I told him all of this. I then told him that the two death wishes of the modern world were Islam and Euro-Socialism. And now we must begin to understand that Jesus is at the Right Hand of the Father.

"You must come back and see me soon...."

Such a gloomy message seems to give hope.

Here is another odd but interesting lesson that I have been through. I met with a city official, and this official likes to talk to me. Maybe it is like Herod liking to hear John the Baptist ("After listening to him he was in great perplexity, and yet he found a pleasure in listening to him." Mark 6:20) or like Felix with Paul ("But when he [Paul] dealt with the subjects of justice, self control, and the judgment which was soon to come, Felix became alarmed..." but he seemed to want the conversations).

I decided on that day not to try to find common ground but to just honor God before this person in my heart and see where it went. I ended up laying it on pretty thick about the coming doom and collapse, the end of an era, the decline of the US and how the decline of marriage and the rise in sexual decadence spelled certain collapse of social energy (the J.D. Unwin thesis[178]). Only Jesus Christ can renew the city throughout the world. Jehovah is the only hope. This person commented on "how depressing" my outlook was. I thought to myself, "Well, this is the last time I will see this person." I went on a lot about covenants coming to an end and how we were the end of an age; and how of modernity had run out of steam (which no longer is able to muster any real belief in anything). I said the Living God is the only hope, and the city can only be renewed through the Church in every city as the true city in the city.

This person (a progressive liberal) finally had to go. As this person stood to go, the hand was extended to shake mine, and then this person said, "I love talking to you. You always give me hope."

This wasn't sarcasm. I have seen this before, and I try

---

178 "Sometimes a man has been heard to declare that he wishes both to enjoy the advantage of high culture and to abolish compulsory continence. The inherent desire of the human organism, however, seems to be such that these desires are incompatible, or even contradictory. Any human society is free to choose either to display great energy or to enjoy sexual freedom: the evidence is that it cannot do both for more than one generation."

J. D. Unwin, *Sex and Culture* (London: Oxford University Press, 1934) p 412

not to forget. Being a prophet of doom and telling people we are under judgment oddly can give them hope.

I was amazed. But why should I have been? I am pretty thick in the head sometimes. Honoring God before the world sometimes works.

Pastors have authority that they are not even aware of, and they can give strength, encouragement and direction that nobody else can, and this can come in odd ways. It can come through a call to understand that we are under judgment. This is a new part of the calling that we have on our shoulders as representatives of The Kingdom of God. Go thou and do likewise. You can.

Doctor Richard Bledsoe